Praise for *Orishas, Goddesses, and*

"Lilith Dorsey writes from her heart
service as a priestess of the divine fem
readers to seek a 'house' and trustwort whom to seek
initiation, she also gives clear instructions and suggestions for ritual practices that anyone can use to experience these beautiful African goddesses and spirits. I'm sure her words will inspire new generations of seekers and priestesses who are exploring their own paths to spirituality."

—Sallie Ann Glassman, author of *Vodou Visions*

"Lilith Dorsey opens the door and shines a light upon the world of African Traditional Religions and their magnificent deities of the divine feminine. Her exceptional storytelling, delicious recipes, offerings, and appendixes give the reader instant access for working properly and respectfully with the orishas, goddesses, and Voodoo queens who are frequently misunderstood or misinterpreted. This book is a must-have for anyone seeking practical and authentic knowledge on how to begin their journey into the multifaceted world of African Traditional Religions. I truly enjoyed it. It is a fantastic read and a book I shall return to many times. Ayibobo!"

—Najah Lightfoot, author of *Good Juju*

"In *Orishas, Goddesses, and Voodoo Queens*, Lilith Dorsey takes readers on an exploratory journey of a beautiful religious current, examining its history, evolution, and even its most complex and uncomfortable aspects, such as slavery, syncretism, and cultural prejudices. The book also includes the most curious recipes and interesting anecdotes, all summed up in one accessible read."

—Elhoim Leafar, author of *The Magical Art of Crafting Charm Bags*

"Applying what resonates most with self on one's spiritual journey is what has worked for me over the years. Lilith Dorsey has created a divine companion, *Orishas, Goddesses, and Voodoo Queens,* for seekers to turn to in their practices. Dive into this treasure chest of a book and learn various gems including spells, rituals, and incantations."

—Riva Nyri Précil, artist, dancer, songstress, and author of *Anaëlle ak Lasirèn*

"Anyone who explores the many witch traditions has their must-have/go-to book. Well, *Orishas, Goddesses, and Voodoo Queens* will become that book for many of you, whatever path or tradition you follow. Packed with rare insight, recipes, and extensive lore regarding each orisha and deity of the African and Caribbean paths, it discusses how they affected our lives in the past and present and how to effectively work with them. It's about darn time. Lilith Dorsey has written a must-read primer for anyone interested in learning about the many dark goddesses. You've got to read this book and learn from one of the best. This will become one of our go-to books at the academy."

—Starr RavenHawk, founder of the New York City Wiccan Family Temple, the WFT Academy of Pagan Studies, and WitchsFest USA

"In *Orishas, Goddesses, and Voodoo Queens,* Lilith Dorsey has created a long-overdue, welcome, and helpful guide for all those interested in goddess, lwa, and orisha work. Dorsey's book is a gift. It presents a concentrated dose of information on select entities, thereby instilling a deep understanding of several figures key to our spirituality. This book not only aids in the understanding of the Divine Feminine of the Motherland and African Diaspora, but it also helps us interact through herbal connections, rituals, altars, prayers and invocations, storytelling, special food recipes, and so much more. Ase!"

—Stephanie Rose Bird, author of *Sticks, Stones, Roots, and Bones*

"Every now and then a book comes along that fills a much-needed void in the literature, and Lilith Dorsey's *Orishas, Goddesses, and Voodoo Queens* does exactly that. One of scant few authors to include New Orleans Voudou in the discussion of African-derived traditions in the United States, Dorsey provides a useful guide to the spirits and queens whose stories and roles have been historically understated in these various religions. More importantly, she tackles the topic from a woman's perspective, when the current social climate is ripe for women's empowerment. This book is a practical guide for working with the energies of the divine feminine in a way that taps into an ancient well of mysteries while remaining accessible to all. I highly recommend Lilith Dorsey's *Orishas, Goddesses, and Voodoo Queens* for anyone who is interested in the stories and backgrounds of these spirits, for anyone who wishes to work with them through ritual and divination, and for all those looking to honor and amplify the sacred and divine feminine energy within themselves."

—Denise Alvarado, author of *The Magic of Marie Laveau* and *The Voodoo Hoodoo Spellbook*

"Emotional and inspiring. Lilith Dorsey's *Orishas, Goddesses, and Voodoo Queens* powerfully exalts the African goddess and elevated beings, as well as illuminates the continual manifestations that grow throughout their vast Diaspora. This is sacred work—to combine this with hands-on formulas for the reader to immerse themselves in is invaluable. *Orishas, Goddesses, and Voodoo Queens* is a one-of-a-kind book and a must-have, a truly unique piece of work that has arrived at a crucial time."

—Witchdoctor Utu, author of *Conjuring Harriet "Mama Moses" Tubman and the Spirits of the Underground Railroad*

ORISHAS, GODDESSES, AND VOODOO QUEENS

• • • • • • • • • • • • • • • • • •

The Divine Feminine in the African Religious Traditions

LILITH DORSEY

WEISER BOOKS

This edition first published in 2020 by Weiser Books, an imprint of
Red Wheel/Weiser, LLC
With offices at:
65 Parker Street, Suite 7
Newburyport, MA 01950
www.redwheelweiser.com

ISBN: 978-1-57863-695-2
Library of Congress Cataloging-in-Publication Data available upon request.

Cover design by Kathryn Sky-Peck
Cover photograph © Hero Images / Getty
Interior by Deborah Dutton
Typeset in Adobe Jensen Pro and Frutiger LT Std

Printed in the United States of America
IBI
10 9 8 7 6 5 4 3 2 1

To Dr. John, aka Mac Rebennack (November 20, 1941–June 6, 2019)

Many knew the musician and the legend, but Mac was more of a father to me than my own ever was. I worked with him, I danced with him, I laughed with him, I performed rituals with him, and above all I loved him. There's so much to thank Dr. John for, not least for making Voodoo bold, beautiful, and always in the rite place at the rite time. I'm sorry I couldn't get to give him one more hug, but so glad I got to tell him how much I loved him. Anywhere and everywhere you are now, Mac, I want to thank you for letting this little brown karakter walk on gilded splinters, and thank u for being you.

I love myself when I am laughing . . . and then again when I am looking mean and impressive.

—Zora Neale Hurston

CONTENTS

Introduction 1

1 Get in Touch with the Goddesses, the Queens, and Your Own Divine Self 17

2 Oshún, the River of Beauty and Love 33

3 Yemaya, the Ocean of Motherly Love 55

4 Oya, the Power of the Wind 67

5 Nana Buruku, the Wisdom of the Ancients 79

6 Mami Wata, the Mother of Wealth 85

7 Erzulie, the Sweet Waterfall of Passion and the Storm of Love 95

8 Aida Wedo, the Shining Crown of the Rainbow 109

9 La Sirene, the Song of Destiny, and Ayizan, the Priestess of Place 119

10 Annie Christmas and Maman Brigitte: New-World Strength and Confidence 131

11 Marie Laveau and the Voodoo Queens 147

12 Pomba Gira and Santa Muerte: Death and the Crossroads 165

Conclusion 183

Acknowledgments 187

Appendix A: Herbs for the Orishas, Loas, and Goddesses 189

Appendix B: Sacred Dirts and Crystals 209

Appendix C: Sacred Symbols 213

Glossary 215

Recommended Resources and Readings 221

INTRODUCTION

I believe this is a vital work for goddess spirituality and feminism whose time is long overdue. Interest in both African traditional religions and women's issues are stronger than ever before, and rightfully so. People look to women of color to elucidate the intersectionality of these topics, and I have dedicated my life to presenting them here, rooting the material in serious scholarship and decades of work in these powerful spiritual traditions.

One of the most important things about the religions that honor the orishas and the loas is their focus on women, and women's empowerment, in traditional and time-honored ways. The orishas and the loas, depending on who is doing the explaining, are cosmic forces in the universe—sometimes personified, sometimes thought of as deities, but always divine. History has not been herstory, and modern women seriously need ways to connect with, and understand, their ancestral warrior strengths and power. *Orishas, Goddesses, and Voodoo Queens* helps to illuminate these powers through stories, spells, and correspondences. Many of these vital qualities are not traditionally thought of as belonging to the warrior; however, the African traditions have a different view. The orisha Oshún, for example, is known to save the world with her sensual beauty. And the orisha Yemaya nurtures and protects mankind so everyone can prosper. We'll investigate the sacred legacies of these goddesses and many more.

There has never before been a book of this kind, and I welcome the opportunity to share this material based on thirty years of scholarship and practice in these traditions. An exciting and an extreme time is now upon us. History has a long list of orishas, loas, goddesses, warrior women, and queens who have embodied the sacred feminine from the dawn of time. These can serve as wise teachers from the past, helping us to navigate an empowered future. In fact, there is nothing that can't be accomplished with the assistance of these forces, as they hold the keys to the ancient mysteries of life itself. One of my spiritual elders likes to remind me that the original mystery was not one of death, but of birth. Birth is a slow and secret process. The orishas, loas, and goddesses nurture physical, emotional, and spiritual births on every level, just as they continually nurture us.

Like many young girls, when I began my spiritual journey, I was hungry for these inspirational feminine deities and all the important lessons they had for me. I also sought out the lessons of the strong women in my family who had come before me. Our ancestors were women who fought for the right to vote, for civil rights, for equality on every level. Even the strong women in our recent memory lived through the Depression, the Cold War, and the sexual revolution to become the resilient foremothers of later generations. They drew their strengths from wherever and however they could find them. Their struggles were real, just as ours are today.

Growing up, I came to know firsthand the challenges my grandmothers and so many other grandmothers suffered trying to craft a better tomorrow for their children. They struggled for equality, for independence, for freedom, and in many cases for their own lives. When I first went to college, I was met with a male-dominated faculty who denied or ignored the contributions of the divine feminine in history and culture. I wish I could say that I was surprised. In one particular dubious instance, I even had an ignorant professor go so far as to say there was no such thing as witches or magick existing in modern society. I longed to prove him wrong, and to responsibly document the reality I had come to know and love. I did this then, as now, not only for myself, but for my daughters who deserved to genuinely know the indomitable legacy they were entitled to inherit. There is a whole battery of feminine strengths that they could draw on from not only the Western world but Africa as well.

This book is designed to unlock and unfold the great mysteries of the ancient and powerful feminine realms of magick. Many are familiar with the warrior goddesses of Greece and Rome (some even made it into pop culture and comics like *Wonder Woman*); but equally important are the divine feminine forces that hail from Africa, even if their story has not been as brightly lit. The appeal of the goddess is rooted in ancient tradition and bolstered by a truly radical feminism. I'll share how to celebrate both the masculine and feminine traits within—and how to foster these traits, gaining strength, improvement, and empowerment in all areas of your life. This book offers magickal solutions, as well as practical, mundane ones. Here you will find spells, rituals, potions, recipes, sacred offerings, and much more to help guide you on your transformational journey.

Most importantly, this book will unfold the divine mysteries of these goddesses—powerful forces like the orisha of the river, Osun (Oshún), of Nigeria; Oya, the orisha of the wind, a superior horsewoman and equal to any man in battle; Voodoo priestess Marie Laveau, who used her powers of persuasion (and some might even say creative "blackmail" of politicians and sex workers) to gain and keep her status; and the divine Nana Buruku, who bolstered her warrior strength with insight from wisdom and age. No matter how they showcase it, each of the goddesses presented here has her own unique qualities to help her survive and thrive in every imaginable situation.

Like the history of women themselves, African traditional religions have often been a victim of suppression, persecution, demonization, and misinformation. Time-honored religions like Ifa, Haitian Vodou, New

Orleans Voodoo, Hoodoo and Conjure, Candomble, Umbanda, and La Regla Lucumi (sometimes mistakenly referred to as Santeria) have frequently been maligned and associated with the darker side of magick, like hexes and curses. In reality, when examining the day-to-day practices, nothing could be further from the truth. There was certainly a history of very unfortunate circumstances that included evils such as slavery and lynching, which did force the religions to offer effective solutions to these horrible injustices. In spite of this, in these dismal realms they grew and flourished. Consequently, these religions and pantheons became supremely strong. I heard an Ifa priest say recently that one of the beautiful things about African traditional religions is that, like a fractal, they can make themselves as small or as large as they need to be. We can carry them in our pockets, or spread them out like a blanket of blessings over our whole community. We can draw on these strengths in every way to continue to empower ourselves today in a modern context.

Enslaved Africans were transported to what colonizers referred to as the "New World" beginning in the 1500s. They were brought by the French, English, Spanish, Dutch, Portuguese, and others to many different parts of the Caribbean, as well as South and North America. By some estimates, over twelve million African people were forcibly shipped away from their homeland during the slave trade. Their stories, their journeys, and their existence in the New World included all levels of horror, torture, and oppression.

In many cases, they were separated from their friends and family, and several countries forbid them from speaking in their native language, reading, writing, singing, dancing, and practicing their traditional religions. However, these religions did not disappear. They were hidden, transformed, and transported in order to be able to survive under the most difficult of conditions.

The African traditional religions—both in their homeland, and in all the places they traveled to—were forced to remain shrouded in secrecy. This was to keep both the practitioners and the knowledge they possessed safe from persecution. The veil of mystery has only just begun to lift after almost five hundred years. In areas like Haiti and Jamaica, the respective religions of Vodou and Obeah have only just started to be recognized by the governments there, and many are still wary of going public with their beliefs. These stigmas have left a legacy of oppression and prejudice that will take a long time to subside.

Due to the nature of slavery, the records that survive from the time are incomplete at best. Hundreds of years have passed, and very often colonizers didn't even take note of where their captives came from. However, scholars have been able to piece together some things about the transport.

It is known that slaves were taken from many different areas of West and Central Africa. Genetic testing can give us a rough idea of some of these histories. In Haiti, the birthplace of Vodou, many of the people who were transported there came from countries now referred to as the Democratic Republic of the Congo, Benin, and Nigeria. In Cuba, the home of the La Regla Lucumi tradition, a large majority of the slaves were taken from Angola, Democratic Republic of the Congo, and Nigeria. The United States saw its slaves come from Gambia, Senegal, Mali, Ghana, Angola, and the Democratic Republic of the Congo. In all the areas, slaves were mixing with the indigenous people, who were also oppressed and often enslaved by the very same colonizers. Just as these individuals came together, so did their magick.

We can only imagine what nightmares these individuals must have endured. Being taken from their homes, sold, abused, raped, tortured, and in some cases murdered. My heart grows very heavy when I think about these atrocities. They left a legacy of ancestral pain that will be felt forever. However, they also left a legacy of resistance. One way this powerful resistance manifested was in the form of powerful religions. Like it or not, adversity can often create opportunity. These African traditional religions grew stronger in response to these extreme hardships.

In addition to secrecy, syncretism was one of the ways that the religions could continue for all these years. Syncretism is the blending of different traditions, religious or otherwise. One of the most puzzling things for people both inside and outside the traditions of Voodoo and La Regla Lucumi is the inclusion of iconography from other religions. I have spoken to many elders who report that one of the main reasons for this was to allow the practices to remain literally under cover.

The most common form of syncretism in Haitian Vodou, New Orleans Voodoo, and La Regla Lucumi in Cuba and Puerto Rico was the use of Catholic saint statues on shrines and during celebrations. Traditionally, these statues were hollow, which allowed the practitioners to put sacred items from their own religions up into the cover of Christianity. This way it looked like people were worshiping the statue, while they were also honoring the contents. For a long time, this was necessary to avoid prejudice and persecution.

There was, however, also a mixing of traditions to some extent. This stems from, I believe, the cosmology of the religions and their belief in the divine power of all things, highlighted under their concept of Ashe. Ashe is explained as the universal life force of Afro-Caribbean religions. Absolutely everything and everyone has Ashe: I have Ashe, you have Ashe, the trees and rocks outside your front door have Ashe. The orisha Oshún, for example, has her own unique Ashe, which is present in the river, in her sacred honey, in her favorite herbs, like cinnamon, in gold, and most especially in the spirit of her children, or devotees.

Under the circumstances, it is a very short leap to see how individuals forced to use St. Lazarus, for example, to represent the orisha Babaluaiye, would choose to also honor and incorporate the healing miracles of this saint. This blending had its roots in colonial times but is still in use today. I have a godson who honors both St. Lazarus and Babaluaiye each year to ensure the continued health of his family. This involves making offerings to the orisha and participating in his local church's processionals and services for the saint. I realize some people may find these practices puzzling, but for many this dual worship allows them to connect with the divine in multiple ways.

Syncretism also manifests with the use of psalms and prayers in traditions like Hoodoo and New Orleans Voodoo. These Christian words allowed followers to worship under the cover of language. In many countries the Bible was the only book slaves were permitted to own. Many believe that this practice of reciting psalms is still used today because there is power in the words, in the mere sound of the words even, which transcends systems and ideologies.

Some have likened the orishas and loas in these systems to gods and goddesses. While I understand the comparison, many staunch followers of African traditional religions dispute this. For them, there is still only one supreme God, viewed as the same one worshiped in Christianity. In Haitian Vodou, He/She is referred to as Bon Dye, or Good God who oversees all things. The same is also true for many followers of La Regla Lucumi, who also identify as having only one God, sometimes identified as Olodumare or Olorun. As I have mentioned before, each house, and in many ways each individual, worships in their own personalized way. In my opinion, each of these is equally valid, and as long as one is under the guidance of a respected spiritual family, each one is correct.

How to get in touch with the orishas, goddesses, queens, and your own divine self will be the focus of Chapter 1. This chapter will discuss simple, yet effective ways for setting up a personal shrine or altar. The importance of cleaning and consecrating your sacred space with traditional herbs, incense, oils, and spells will be explored. We will delve into the powers of the goddesses that can be strengthened and intensified by exploring our own divine nature and attributes. The importance of connecting with the divine feminine both through ritual and divination with items such as tarot cards or a pendulum will also be stressed. A complete calendar is also included, so you can celebrate your feasts and holy days along with the rest of the world. This will give you a firm foundation as you travel down your spiritual path.

One of the most powerful and beautiful forces in the African traditional religions is known as Oshún. She is the focus of Chapter 2. Called by many different names (Osun, Oshún, Oxun, Oxum, or Ochun, depending on the area), she is representative of the Ashe, or sacred energy, of the river. Hers is a sweet river of tears cried in joy, and sometimes in sorrow, that is capable of blessing our true souls. She illustrates the principle that love is always stronger than hate. Many don't think of her as a warrior goddess, because unlike some of the orishas and goddesses who actually do have conventional battle skills, her strength comes shining through in her sensuality and beauty. The most famous pataki, or sacred divination tale, about her tells of how she saved the entire world with her seductive powers of persuasion. According to most versions of the story, a group of menstruating women had threatened to take over the world. Neither the orisha Ogun, with his military power, nor the orisha Chango, with his drums and sacred fire, could stop them. The world was at a loss until Oshún, with her seductive dancing and sweet honey from her luscious hips, could persuade these women to do otherwise. This story artfully illustrates how divine power and warrior strength can take many forms besides brute force and violent conflict. Oshún rightfully claims as her sacred domain love, marriage, money (specifically gold), dancing, fertility, and abundance in their highest manifestation. She is envisioned by some as the ultimate personification of beauty in all its forms. Throughout time, her true mysteries have remained artfully cloaked due to the secrecy of initiation and practice. There are, however, many ways to honor and connect with this lovely orisha, even if traditional avenues of study are immediately unavailable. We will detail these in this chapter, including simple herbs, offerings, spells, recipes, and rituals to better understand and contact the energy of this sacred orisha.

Chapter 3 focuses on the orisha Yemaya. Occupying the role of divine mother, Yemaya has great strength. Her name means "mother whose children are the fish of the sea." The Ashe of the ocean is what we find in her. She is honored with salt baths, oils made with the treasures of the sea, and other watery ritual offerings that we will discuss and explore. Yemaya can graciously grant the bounty of the ocean, or send crashing waves if you are not adequately prepared for her presence. Many newcomers to African traditional religions recognize Yemaya as similar to the Mother Goddess, or even the Virgin Mary. She encompasses all these elements and much more.

With electric sparks shooting from her spiky hair and a scream in her heart, the orisha Oya presents a more classic picture of the warrior goddess. Chapter 4 focuses on this sacred force who is the embodiment of the wind. She stands side by side with her husband Chango to fight all who would challenge the pair. Oya is the very air of life. Many perceive her as a queen of the ancestors, whose ritual place is found in the cemetery. Some scholars have argued that she is an amalgam of Native American and European goddesses combined with traditional African notions of female divinity. Whatever cultural threads make up her multicolored skirt, she manifests as a powerful force. Oya possesses the powers of shape-shifting and its related component of invisibility. Her representations are known to be both strong and sexual. Ways to access her power—through gris-gris bags, candles, oils, recipes, and more—will be examined in this chapter.

Chapter 5 is dedicated to Nana Buruku. As a fierce, strong, and powerful protector of women, Nana Buruku is a goddess for these terribly trying times. In a way she almost transcends time itself, as one of the oldest energies in the orisha pantheon. One of my dearest friends is an Ifa priest, or *babalawo*, and in his opinion Nana Buruku is beyond the constraints of time, full of sacred inspiration spawned across the ages, and cloaked in mystery and silence. Even her sacred tools are created entirely of wood, as if her weaponry predates even Bronze Age tools, weapons, and technology. She teaches us about survival through a deep and commanding wisdom, the knowledge of our great-grandmothers, and all the women in the line who have come before. Honoring her through offerings, spells, and shrines is covered in this chapter.

Mami Wata also occupies the space of ancient and powerful creator. Chapter 6 explores her realms of deep, watery knowledge and bounty.

Found throughout central and coastal Africa, she is one of the oldest entities in existence, with evidence from the fifteenth century and before. Mami Wata is most often depicted as a beautiful woman on the top and a fish on the bottom. She presents as seductive and generous, yet also sometimes jealous or dangerous. Her primal wisdom and gifts will be explored with magic waters, recipes, rituals, and rites in this chapter.

In the island nation of Haiti, many of the sacred energies shifted as they traveled on the beaten backs of enslaved people transported from Africa. Many of the people of color who were taken to Haiti came from Dahomey, a kingdom in western Africa. Accordingly, the deities they took with them reflect these fierce tribal ties. Today, in Haitian Vodou one of the most prominent loas, or sacred forces, is the goddess Erzulie. Chapter 7 focuses on the myriad loas who fall under the name Erzulie. With an infinite number of manifestations, she shares with us every aspect of love and feminine power. There is Erzulie Freda Dahomey, who cries tears for the sadness and shortcomings of humanity. She is perfumed, coquettish, and full of compassion. This is in direct contrast to Erzulie Danto, a more typical feminine warrior who is a commanding protector of children, abused women, and victims of domestic violence. Erzulie Taureau is associated with the bull, and has been known to mount her devoted followers just like a bull. A fierce and ancient grandmother comes to us as Erzulie Mapyang. Yet in all her beautiful forms, Erzulie is the Ashe and spirit of the waterfall. There are many different ways to honor her, including through the use of oils, waters, baths, spells, and recipes contained in chapter 7.

Haiti is also home to the sacred serpent and the rainbow whose mythology has become famous throughout the entire world. This rainbow serpent, Aida Wedo, is the focus of the eighth chapter. Snake goddesses are as old as time and tide, echoing the sacred beginnings that gave birth to us all. Aida Wedo is a divine wife, bride, mother, and progenitor, and a beacon of hope. Her warrior strength springs forth from this hope, which urges us to believe things can always improve, just like a magical rainbow after a storm. Here we dance with the unbelievable power of believing. It is a dance of the ancestors, those women and men who carried on despite and against all odds. Furthermore, it is a dance of potential that urges us toward a new hope and a better tomorrow.

Like many of the other orishas and loas featured here, Aida Wedo is a formidable force that we can draw on in our daily lives. Connecting to this goddess takes supreme patience and fortitude—important traits to have when befriending any snake. Equally important is skill. Luckily, rituals and recipes to tap into this wisdom are highlighted in chapter 8.

The focus of chapter 9 is two more loas primarily from the Haitian Vodou pantheon—namely, La Sirene and Ayizan. The divine feminine is ever present in this tradition, and this is embodied in two of the most well-known loas: La Sirene, the watery mistress who sings songs from beyond, and Ayizan, the grand priestess who guides the religion and its followers through time immemorial. La Sirene (also called Lasirèn, Lasireen, and La Sirenn) is part of the Rada family of loa in Haitian Vodou, and her watery domain is the sea. She helps us to navigate the boundaries between truth and illusion, fantasy and reality. Ayizan is considered to be the first mambo, or priestess, of Haitian Vodou, whose spirit lives on in all the mambos that have followed. Ayizan can provide invaluable guidance when an individual is seeking or undergoing initiation. Offerings, songs, shrines, spells, rites, and recipes for La Sirene and Ayizan are included in this chapter.

One of the most fascinating things about the African traditional religions is that, as living and continuous systems, they are constantly evolving to meet the demands of a devout audience. People learn and progress in these religions in a complex system of study involving priests and priestesses that function as godparents to individuals in the tradition. Through tribute and participation, the individuals and the religions themselves gain strength. It is in this process that new loas and orishas can emerge. This is more common in Haiti and New Orleans than in other areas of African diasporic religion.

New Orleans has seen the creation of many deified individuals over the years. Arguably, the most prominent is Voodoo queen Marie Laveau.

She is joined by Annie Christmas, another powerful ancestor spirit who is still honored today. These two women, in addition to the relatively recent loa Maman Brigitte, make up the magical focus of chapter 10.

Marie Laveau was a legend and a goddess in her own time, just as she is today. As the first woman to hold open public spiritual services in New Orleans, she expanded the power and scope of the Voodoo religion, and it is said that even Queen Victoria was one of her clients. Marie Laveau is said to grant wisdom, peace, supreme justice, and protection to all those who seek it. She triumphed against a multitude of odds with an arsenal of warrior skills and tactics. In this chapter you will find ritual waters, gris-gris bags, recipes, shrines, and sacred rituals all designed to help you connect with the divine force that is the legendary Voodoo queen Marie Laveau.

Annie Christmas is another nineteenth-century woman who, like Marie Laveau, lived in New Orleans. Colorful urban legends tell us that she was an engineer on the railroads and streetcars in the city. She worked side by side with the men in the muck and mire. Annie Christmas's lasting legacy and great strength ensured that she was a force to be remembered and reckoned with even today. Chapter 10 will show ways to honor Annie Christmas with offerings and more to draw upon her energy whenever needed.

The New Orleans Voodoo tradition was also where loas like Maman Brigitte were allowed to develop and flourish. This goddess is also known as Mademoiselle Brigitte, or Gran Brigitte. Many see her as an outcropping of religious syncretism, or blending, that occurred when Irish immigrants brought their worship of the goddess and saint Brighid to the United States and Caribbean. Like Brighid, Maman Brigitte possesses the power over sacred fire. Where she differs, however, is that she is seen as queen of the cemetery. Oils, gris-gris bags, and offerings for her will be discussed in chapter 10.

The modern world has become a magical melting pot, for better or worse. I had intended for the last chapter of this book to be dedicated to goddesses throughout the rest of the world—those from the Celtic,

Native American, Central American, South American, and Norse pantheons. Our global sphere becomes closer every day, and by adding these goddesses I intended to illustrate that the divine power of the sacred feminine wears many faces. However, as I began the editing process, I quickly became convinced that this book should focus solely on the sacred feminine as it manifests in the African diaspora. Goddesses like Lilith, Hecate, Freya, and Hel inspire me daily, but this book must have a narrower focus, one on deities who have often taken a back seat to those common in literature and scholarship. To that end, the final chapter of this book focuses on the sacred feminine in the form of Brazil's Pomba Giras, and Mexico's Santa Muerte. The Pomba Giras are mistresses of the crossroads, the in-between spaces where magick and mystery reside. Santa Muerte has, especially lately, become the darling face of death for many followers throughout the world. Her roots are in Mexico and this Lady is worshiped by several Latinx individuals everywhere.

The appendixes provide a handy guide to all the herbs, crystals, and symbols referred to throughout the book. This will be very useful as you tailor your own magickal workings and offerings. It will help you to connect with the sacred goddess energy in your own life to bring about positive change and success. Sometimes an individual, especially one with psychic power, finds themselves drawn to a particular plant, animal, or gemstone. I encourage you to explore those connections, and how they might offer clues to unlocking the energy of different goddesses and the roles they have to play in your life. Maybe you have a strong connection to amber or sunflowers; this might point to the influence of Oshún, who has these as some of her sacred offerings. Alternatively, maybe the language of the raven calls to you, which can be a signal of the goddess Hecate and that sublime warrior energy in your life. All of the items mentioned throughout the book will be chronicled here for use as needed. There is also a glossary, which will guide you through questions you may have about pronunciation or unfamiliar words and concepts.

The information provided in these pages is helpful not only for women, but for men and other genders as well. Particularly those who have inspirational women as mothers, lovers, daughters, or friends, and also want to strengthen their own feminine side will hopefully find something special and useful in these pages. The sacred feminine runs through every facet of life, and this book is designed to explore those forces on every level. We will examine these powerful feminine forces from Africa, beyond, and back, and show how connection with them can help shape and change our lives for the better on every front.

There is no cure-all magick that is suitable for everyone. Just as some people have deadly allergies, some practices will be dangerous to certain individuals, and imperative for others. Magickal healing takes all forms. This book is not meant to be a substitute or shortcut to initiation, or enlightenment, but rather a helpful supplement to it. I cannot stress this enough.

Another important issue that arises when discussing these orishas, loas, and goddesses is that while there are many accepted practices regarding these divine forces, each spiritual house is unique and will have its own rules and regulations. Like the process of cooking, some people have their favorite recipe for a treasured family dish, perhaps handed down for generation upon generation. These concoctions may be different from person to person, or location to location. None is wrong, but none is absolutely right, either. You may, hopefully, find one that jives with you. I hope you find a qualified teacher in your spiritual journey who sings to your soul and helps you grow in necessary ways, as my teachers and godparents have always done for me. This book is intended to serve as a guide, not a stand-in for blessings and initiations by a true professional.

The recent interest and popularity of African traditional religions have given rise to many falsehoods and much misinformation. Unfortunately, tools like the internet have only made things worse. I have heard and seen some truly extreme things. This is another reason why initiation is so important. I would never advise someone to do something I hadn't undergone and continue to undergo myself. You must trust and respect your teachers, and instructions for finding a genuinely qualified one will be given in detail. I'm sure there are also those who will disagree with me for even putting any of this knowledge down on paper. African traditional religions have historically been oral traditions. However, the rise of the internet and the historical secrecy surrounding the practices have meant that much has been lost or transformed in negative ways over the years. I recently attended a panel in my hometown of New York City about whether or not it was a good thing to continue to keep the practices hidden. There were discussions on both sides of the issue, with some of the older members of the community reminding us that there was a historical precedent for the safety provided by secrecy. The other side of the debate, however, reminds us that by coming public we are able to correct damaging falsehoods and stereotypes. It is in this humble spirit that I undertake the writing of this book.

This is an exciting journey for me, as I hope it will be for you too. The spells, instructions, recipes, and rituals contained here are based on decades of research and sacred practice with these divine goddesses involving me, my teachers, my students, and my clients. For most of my life as an anthropologist and a ritual practitioner, I have explored the divine energy and power of these sacred goddesses, orishas, loas, and Voodoo queens. They have lovingly seen me through some of the hardest times, and graciously danced me through more joyous ones. May the feminine forces be with you!

1

GET IN TOUCH WITH THE GODDESSES, THE QUEENS, AND YOUR OWN DIVINE SELF

Regardless of our gender, many of us feel a deep connection to the orishas, goddesses, and queens of the African diaspora. Ancient and powerful, inspiring and majestic, they call out to us from deep inside our souls. Even if we are uninitiated, or in the process of becoming more dedicated in the religions, there are ways we can strengthen these connections. This can be done by leaving offerings, setting up sacred shrines, and seeing how the Ashe of these divine beings affect our lives in profound ways.

In the religions of La Regla Lucumi, Haitian Vodou, and New Orleans Voodoo, an individual is seen to be the child of a loa or orisha. The loas and orishas are fiercely protective of their children or initiates. These guiding orishas or loas can be referred to as a mother or father, a head and feet, or in Haitian Kreyol a Ti Bon Ange (Little Good Angel) and Gros Bon Ange (Big Good Angel). Which loa or orisha this is can only be determined through divination, often by multiple priests or priestesses.

In La Regla Lucumi, each individual is believed to have guardian orishas. One does not choose their own guardian orishas; the gods always get to choose you. Some houses conceptualize them as a mother and father parenting you through all aspects of life; some think of them as your head and feet, with one guiding your thoughts, and the other guiding your direction. The only proper way to determine your guardian orishas is through divination and ceremony by multiple babalawos, or high priests. I've heard many stories about people being swindled when looking to find this information, so please actively research who you are dealing with in the religion before you begin. This way you will save yourself much trouble down the line.

It also bears saying that one's loa or orisha can't be divined remotely, or over video chat. Some practitioners even believe that these things can be fluid, and will continue to change until the individual receives proper initiation to seat, crown, or otherwise solidify and elevate the connection between an orisha or loa and themselves.

In choosing godparents or spiritual teachers to help facilitate this connection, there are many factors to consider. Finding godparents is a really complicated process. The religions have been forced to remain secret for so many years, and because of this some less than stellar practices, by some less than stellar characters, unfortunately have been allowed to exist. You could end up with someone who tries to manipulate you, is dishonest financially and spiritually, or even lands you in jail. I have heard of all of these things happening to individuals seeking initiation in African traditional religions. The religions have been forced to remain secret for many years, and because of this some less than stellar practices exist. Given this, I've included a list of questions and concerns you should ponder before embarking on a spiritual journey with someone. Please be respectful and mindful at all times during your process.

Even before you start asking questions directly of a practitioner, consider which form of African traditional religion or other spiritual practice you want to join. The world is a spiritual cornucopia. Common African traditional religions include, but are not limited to, Ifa, La Regla Lucumi, Haitian Vodou, New Orleans Voodoo, Palo, 21 Divisions, Hoodoo and Conjure, Candomble, Umbanda, and more. While there are some vague similarities, each one is delightfully unique and different. You can learn more about these religions by reading this book, my first book, *Voodoo and Afro-Caribbean Paganism,* and some of the works suggested in the "Recommended Resources and Readings."

Once you've determined which religion interests you most, do not walk into an establishment or temple and demand an initiation. Respectfully find out what you can. Perhaps consider getting a reading; most likely this will inform how you proceed.

At the start of your journey I also suggest discussing the godparent's spiritual lineage. Who are or were your teacher's teachers? What influences do your teachers have? Some houses don't traditionally give out an entire lineage, but this is something you should definitely have access to if you are thinking about joining a spiritual house and starting to complete your own initiations. The systems function on an intricate interplay between teacher and student at every level imaginable. There is no guidebook or bible for these religions; they are instead handed down from person to person.

You should also find out exactly what will be required of you if you initiate with this house. These commitments are serious and should not be taken lightly. Will you have to attend rites and ceremonies? Will there be financial commitments? Each individual house is different, and also correct. I cannot stress this enough. Every house has its own unique requirements for godchildren that may even change from person to person. In the La Regla Lucumi house I started in, we were required to abide by the reading of the year, keep our personal and house obligations, and participate in house events, either financially or in person—and in an ideal world both. One thing that also comes as a shock to those outside the community is that many of the rites and initiations come with a hefty price tag. Some say this is in lieu of a tithe, or an actual full-time apprenticeship, which may have been more common in the past.

The other thing to consider is that once you have joined a house, leaving it can be as difficult if not more difficult than separating yourself from your blood family. I know one woman who set out to initiate with a Haitian Vodou house, only to find after she had completed the ceremonies that she did not agree to all that she had promised. I'm still unclear as to if the problem was due to a language barrier or what, but I do know she spent many years trying to separate herself from that spiritual family, and still suffers from problems as a consequence.

Another logistical thing you need to establish is both how and when you communicate with your godparent or teacher. Your teachers are people too, and some will prefer to do business via telephone, in person, or over social media. It's best to establish these things up front. Otherwise you may not receive the answers or guidance you seek in a timely fashion. Everyone's problems are of the utmost importance to them, but realize some spiritual leaders are responsible for the well-being of dozens of individuals and their extended families.

As you can already see, the sacred houses of African traditional religion most often operate like a family. You have spiritual godparents, and also spiritual godbrothers and godsisters. More often than not, these are like regular sibling relationships with ups and downs. In my own spiritual house I encourage my godchildren to speak and interact with newcomers and each other, so everyone can help and benefit each other. When considering joining a house, ask if you can meet some of the other participants there. They may be able to answer questions that you have about this chosen path.

During this process, I would also consider asking what your godparent's positions are on controversial topics such as animal sacrifice, homosexuality, etc. If their practices are against your beliefs, you can see how this could quickly become a problem. Along the way I would also be mindful of your prospective godparent's character. Are they prone to addictive behavior? Are they constantly fighting with those in the community? Their elders? Or even their own godchildren? Get a sense of them as a person, and see if the relationship will truly be able to flourish. In many ways these relationships will tell you about the character of the person and their spiritual house.

It's not only your teachers you should question before you begin studying. You should also ask some hard questions of yourself. In many ways this is just as, if not more, important. There are no real shortcuts in life or in spirituality, so if you are serious about connecting with the orisha or loa, beginning ceremonies and most likely initiation are necessary. Ask yourself if you have the time and/or energy to devote to these practices. They can mean daily or weekly offerings, readings, participation in rituals and events, and possibly more. Very often I meet people who tell me they don't have the time necessary to devote to Santeria or Voodoo. My response is usually, "How do you not have time to better your life?" Devotion to these traditions can bring rewards greater than you could imagine. They can help you avoid unnecessary trouble and find your joy. You must, however, start out on the proper path. This doesn't mean everything will come easy to you, but hopefully it means your lessons will come as gently and clearly as possible.

As the Yoruba proverb says, "You can't get Awo from a book." *Awo* translates as "spiritual knowledge" or "mysterious power." There is no substitute in the African diasporic traditions for proper guidance from a godmother and godfather. They are there to help guide you through the complexities of the religion, and of your life. They are to be consulted regularly for direction, clarity, and blessing. Anyone serious about the religion should do all they can to find a spiritual house to join and study with. In some cases, this won't be easy. I have to travel over a thousand miles to be with my spiritual family, but it is worth it, and that's how it is done. The beginning rituals in the religion are seen to give insight and clarity. They allow for recognition by the orisha, and until then it is believed that you are working outside the guidelines of the tradition, and anything can happen.

Altars and Shrines

In African diasporic tradition much emphasis is placed on altars and shrines. Just to clarify, an altar is a temporary space created to bring about a desired change, while a shrine is a more permanent setup designed to honor a divinity, be it a god, goddess, orisha, or loa. Either one can be a place to worship, pray, leave offerings, or do personal rituals. Almost all the recipes and rituals in this book assume you will have at the very least a basic working altar. This assures that you will have a clean and clear space to create your own magick.

Over the years I have set up over a hundred altars and shrines, and helped hundreds of people set up these sacred spaces for themselves. Try to remember that this is a creative process. There are some useful guidelines to follow, but you can and will be inspired by doing this. At the core of this practice is gratitude. Devotees give thanks for the ancestors, loa, and orisha daily or as often as necessary. With my students I find it particularly helpful to recommend that they try starting their day in front of their altar or shrine with prayers and offerings of gratitude. They may say something along the lines of, "Thank you for blessing me and opening my day," or words of their own choosing. You may wish to incorporate something similar into your own practices.

The process of creating a sacred space most often begins with a clearing and a cleansing working. Cleanliness is paramount in all the African diasporic religions. Items, individuals, and also the space must be clean. The first step to creating an altar will be physically cleansing your entire space. You can use your favorite cleaning products. Some spiritual people are partial to things like ammonia, bleach, vinegar, or laundry bluing. Each creates its own unique type of clean. Ammonia is said to connect with the energy of the wind and the air element, while bleach is seen as a cleaner for everything—a start-fresh-again kind of product. Adding some vinegar to your wash and cleaning water is helpful with averting and banishing unwanted energy. Laundry bluing has been used for over a century to get things both clean and also free from pests and negativity. Whichever method you choose, be sure to vary it from time to time. If you use the same type of cleansing each time, you may notice that it becomes less effective, almost as if the negative energy begins to build up an immunity. So the best practice is to change methods every so often to make sure you are achieving the best results.

Physically cleansing your space will make sure your mind can focus on the tasks at hand without being distracted by dirt or clutter. Uncleanliness and clutter also attract all types of negativity, so if you choose to not deal with those things you are disabling your efforts from the start. If you are unsure on how to proceed and what ingredients to use, please consult the guidelines throughout this book.

Equally as important as cleansing your space is cleansing yourself. There are any number of ways that this can be achieved. You may wish to use sea salt, Florida Water, holy water, or other items to accomplish this. One of my favorite methods simply involves coconut and water.

COCONUT CLEANSING BATH

Ingredients

- 1 fresh coconut, with milk inside
- 1 gallon spring water

Crack open the coconut with a hammer or other tool. Pour the fresh coconut milk out into a large bowl. (If the liquid smells foul or if the inside flesh is slimy, throw it out and get another coconut.) Add the spring water. Standing in your tub or shower, pour the liquid over your head. Then rinse off with cool water. Repeat as often as necessary. This practice is particularly good when you are feeling down or confused. ■

Spiritually Cleansing the Space

The next step is to spiritually cleanse the space. This should be done using all the elements: earth, air, fire, water, and spirit. Each element will loan its own type of blessing to the necessary process. What follows are simple guidelines for doing this in a traditional way. However, if you have your own special blessings for the elements you would like to use, by all means, employ them here.

Earth

For the element of earth, herbs can be easily burnt on charcoal, which also involves the elements of fire and air. It may be easier to do this outdoors, or near an open window or door. You can also add a very small amount of herbs to a candle. Be cautious, however, as using too much can interfere with the burning of your candle. Alternatively, herbs can be added to your ritual water, and a cleansing wash can be made for the area you are working on.

Some people choose to use crystals to represent the element of earth, and stones like black tourmaline and jet are great at removing negative energy and transforming it into something useful for your magick. These can be placed on the altar overnight to help prepare the space. You may also wish to set up crystal grids as part of your protection and cleansing rituals. This involves using sacred geometry and arranging crystals or other items in squares, circles, stars, or other magickal shapes as powerful boundaries and markers for your space. The process can be as simple or as complex as you choose to make it.

One other thing that I often like to do to bring the element of the earth to a ritual space is to include a live plant. Choose one that is good for protection and easy to grow, like basil, aloe or another succulent, or even a peace lily. If you can't use a living plant, consider adding some flowers or greenery as part of your earthy cleansing process. In Haitian Vodou, palm fronds are often placed in the corners and even on the ceiling of a space to cleanse and protect it, while in La Regla Lucumi live plants are often used for the same purpose.

Air

Ritually preparing your space with the element of air very often can involve the use of incense. You may also choose to cleanse your space with a smudge stick or palo santo. If you do go this route, please remember that sage, which is often used in smudge sticks, is not recommended for pregnant or nursing mothers. And palo santo has been heavily harvested in the wild, and is now classified by some environmental organizations as threatened or endangered. Please try to obtain it from a responsible source. When burning incense or smudging, be sure to focus on all the corners of your space, and pay special attention to the doors, windows, and thresholds.

Water

The element of water can be used to cleanse a space and an individual by preparing ritual floor washes and baths. These combine sacred waters, like holy water or rain water, along with essential oils and herbal infusions to bring about a desired effect. If you are making a wash to remove negative energy and protect your space, both the stirring of the mixture and the washing of the space should be carried out in a counterclockwise motion. By literally stirring things up in this direction, you will help to remove unwanted energies from the space. After you have used a floor wash for cleansing, it is best to dispose of the wash water outdoors under a large tree. Dump it out, and do not look back.

Fire

I am a fire sign, and fire is hands down my favorite element. Almost all the magick I do incorporates a fire component. The simplest way to incorporate the fire element to bless your space is to use a candle. A small taper or votive candle, covered with some essential oil, is great for a quick and easy blessing. If you prefer something more long lasting, consider using a larger candle, or 7-day removable cylinder in glass. At our home temple, we have one or more 7-day candles going whenever possible. As always, remember to never leave a candle burning unattended. My best advice if you are unable to stay present in the space until your candle is done burning is to say a prayer while you are extinguishing it, snuff it out with a candle snuffer or by some other method, and then relight it and say another prayer as soon as you are able.

Another way of incorporating fire to cleanse a space requires the use of a fireplace. You can add essential oils, herbs, and even written petitions and blessings directly into your fireplace and light it.

Spirit

Last, but certainly not least, it is always advisable to do a spiritual cleansing on your space from time to time. This will involve a combination of the methods we have already discussed, as well as things from your own spiritual repertoire. Maybe you want to bless the space with your ritual wand, or other magickal tool. These types of actions would be highly appropriate. This is your space, and your personal power will help to protect it.

Much of this may seem complicated, but the more time you spend preparing your ritual space, the more successful you will be. Hopefully, you wouldn't invite an honored guest to your home if everything wasn't clean and just right, and the same holds true for the goddesses, orishas, and loas.

Many are familiar with the concept of an ancestor altar or shrine. Spaces like these are obviously not limited to African diasporic traditions—anyone can create a sacred area to honor those who have come before. In New Orleans Voodoo and Haitian Vodou much time and attention are given to the ancestors. Weekly, if not daily, offerings and prayers are respectfully given. Ancestors are given food, drink, candles, money, and more. If enough sincere and proper care is given to those who are gone, they elevate to the realm of honored ancestors—possibly even becoming loas themselves. Some conceive of these loas as saints, or gods, or just representations of divine energy. In any case, they are very powerful, and they can be very helpful to the living if the proper tributes are given. So in addition to remembering that our loved ones are on another level of existence, we also have to remember to help them on their journey so they can continue to help us on ours.

What or whom should you include on your ancestor altar or shrine? This is one area where people seem to take some interesting liberties. Traditionally, your ancestors are those in your direct physical and spiritual family lines. If you have other honored dead you would like to include, that is okay, but know this is a slightly different process.

When people are adopted, they often wonder who they should put in this space. I get this question quite a lot, and the answer is simple. In these situations, it is best to use whatever yes/no divination system works for you. That could be dowsing rods, tarot cards, a pendulum, or whatever other way you prefer. See what names, places, and thoughts come clearly to you, and then test out if they are supposed to go on the shrine with your yes/no method. This will give you a decent place to start creating your altar or shrine.

There is no wrong time to start creating an ancestor altar. However, some people have a special reverence for the dead around Samhain (Halloween). If you don't have a special place for your ancestors set up already, I suggest you make one right away. The logic behind this is that your ancestors were the individuals who cared the most about you in your life, and they will continue to care for you after they have passed. They will help you on your journey to find teachers, build a greater connection to the orishas and goddesses, and achieve overall success. Be sure to include photos of those who have crossed over along with their favorite items. It is also a place to light a devotional candle (do not leave it unattended), and maybe place a glass of water.

In Haitian Vodou and New Orleans Voodoo, almost anything and everything can find a place on this altar or shrine. I've seen everything a person can hold dear placed here, from liquor to cigarettes to jewelry. Sometimes petitions are placed beneath or around the wick of a candle to send messages and requests to those who have passed on. Most common are offerings of money (both coins and cash), liquor, photos, medals, and mass cards. In these traditions they are most often huge creations that span from floor to ceiling. In La Regla Lucumi these spaces are called *bovedas*, which translates to "vault," "safe," "cavern," and "canopy of heaven" (my favorite). It is here that people leave offerings and perform divination with those honored there. Some spiritual houses have bovedas as a standard element, while others do not. Some have them in a separate room, while some even have them in a separate building. If you can, take the opportunity to look at some of these magnificent manifestations online or in person. These will hopefully give you some inspiration for your own creation.

One beautiful form of ancestor shrine created throughout the southern United States is the bottle tree, which is made from brightly colored bottles placed over the branches of a tree (or in more recent years, a metal frame). While it works best to use a dead tree with bare branches, if you are making one from a living tree, focus on the younger branches. These branches are more flexible and will be able to grow along with your tree. The first bottle tree I made grew strong, and even had leaves growing inside of the bottles after a while. Most often people use clear, green, or blue bottles, but any colors will work. Blue is most likely associated with cobalt blue, and haint blue, two colors traditionally used in protection magick. The color is said to appease the spirits. Make sure the bottles are clean and empty; then hang or place them on the ends of the branches. In conclusion, you can add as many or as few bottles as you like, as your list of helpful ancestors is virtually infinite.

In addition to ancestor altars, shrines, bottle trees, and working altars, you may also choose to set up specific shrines for the orishas and goddesses you will be honoring in your spiritual practice. These can be as simple or as elaborate as you wish, and detailed suggestions will be given throughout this book.

A Few Words About Prayer and Offerings

Many years ago, I had the opportunity to be part of an African and African American Interfaith Council. Many different religions were represented. Our meetings occurred not long after the implementation of the start of Catholic Mass being given in US churches in English. This was part of many changes that had occurred in the church to move away from some of the traditional practices. Masses were still given in other languages, but this move made language barriers less of an issue. Our informal conversations in the interfaith council soon ran to this topic. Some of the older devout members disagreed with these changes. My younger self took the position in support of these moves, believing that services in a common language would allow the meaning and the message to be accessible to many more people. Some debates followed. At the time I held my position, but over the years I have come to understand the wisdom of their opinion.

There is a kind of magick and power in certain words. They vibrate with a spiritual frequency. They resonate with the forces in the universe. It isn't only mainstream Christianity that recognizes this benefit; Hoodoo and Conjure spells and workings very frequently use psalms from the Bible as invocations and prayers. Many practitioners view this as less of an allegiance to the Bible, and more of a recognition that the sounds of the words said aloud have the power to help them manifest their desires. There are some spells and rituals here in this book that include a prayer or praise for the orishas or goddesses, and in all those instances you are also free to use a prayer of your own. Your words should always be respectful, genuine, and heartfelt. Now, what do you do if you are unsure of which words to use?

When I first began on my spiritual path of New Orleans Voodoo, I was surprised to see members of the temple doing interesting things with sighs, breaths, and other subtle noises as part of their prayers. I am curious to a fault, so I quickly asked them what that behavior was all about. They explained that something as simple as your breath can always be used as an offering. It comes from deep inside you, and if offered sincerely and humbly, it represents all that is within you. Now I frequently recommend that others use their breath to charge things like magickal oils or items they have created. Doing this is like putting your personal touch on the working. This type of blessing also allows you to consecrate items even when you may not have the traditional ingredients around. Even though there are guidelines, remember everything can be sacred to a divinity in the proper context.

Focusing on the Orishas, Goddesses, and Voodoo Queens

Once you have completed the basic step of setting up your ancestor altar or shrine, you can then focus on creating ritual spaces, leaving offerings, and further honoring the orishas, goddesses, and Voodoo queens in your own home. As I have stated, this can be done whenever necessary, but there are certain times when these energies are traditionally honored with feasts and celebrations. These feast days and celebrations are also a time to reach out to your local community so you can observe these holidays in a traditional way.

Holidays and Other Celebrations

The dates that follow should be seen as guidelines, as different houses will celebrate feasts on different days. This calendar is intended to provide a rough guideline of some of those dates for the orishas, loas, and goddesses discussed here. While I never recommend people wait for a feast day to do necessary magickal work, if you are trying to develop a relationship with a particular goddess, please do your best to remember her at her special times. Please note this list is not exhaustive—just a brief beginning to start you along your way.

January 10: Voodoo holiday in Benin

February 2: Feast for Maman Brigitte in Haitian Vodou and New Orleans Voodoo

May 30: Day for honoring Joan of Arc, who was put to death on May 30, 1431. She is associated with Marinette or Anima Sola in Haitian Vodou.

June 23: St. John's Eve, celebrated in New Orleans Voodoo

June 25: Feast Day for Mami Wata

July 16 or 26: Feast for Nana Buruku in La Regla Lucumi

July 16 corresponds to Our Lady of Mount Carmel, who is sometimes associated with this orisha.

August 11: Day of celebration for Ayizan

August 15: Feast day for Santa Muerte

September 7: Feast of Yemaya in La Regla Lucumi

September 8: Feast of Oshún in La Regla Lucumi. This day corresponds to the Catholic feast day of Our Lady of Charity, also known as Nuestra Senora de la Caridad del Cobre, or the Blessed Virgin Mary.

November 1: Alternate feast day for Santa Muerte

December 31: Brazilian Candomble feast for Iemanja (Yemaya)

Connecting with Tarot and Oracle Decks, and Other Forms of Divination

Throughout this book we will explore many different ways to access the divine power of the sacred feminine. I have done my best to provide detailed information and instructions for honoring these women respectfully. Obviously working with a teacher in person can and will help the process, and you may wish to use divination to help guide you along your path. I highly advise working with a professional psychic you trust (most people don't try to fix their car if they aren't a trained mechanic). But in the event that you are reading for yourself because sometimes you must, you may wish to choose a goddess based on an oracle or tarot deck. Here are a few that I sincerely recommend:

- *The Divine Feminine Oracle* by Meggan Watterson
- *The Goddess Oracle Deck and Book* by Amy Sophia Marashinsky and Hrana Janto
- *The New Orleans Voodoo Tarot* by Louis Martinie and Sallie Ann Glassman
- *Dust II Onyx: A Melanated Tarot* by Courtney Alexander

Connecting with a tarot or oracle deck can give you a deeper understanding of how these goddesses are operating in your life. You can choose one of the goddess cards as a tool for meditation or as a focal point for your altar. I even know some people who like to choose a goddess card to put under their pillow in hopes of inspiring their dreams. This is especially useful when you feel like you are being called to a particular goddess. When you receive a new deck, be sure to consecrate or charge it by leaving it on your working altar or shrine overnight. One of my spiritual teachers also recommends making a meal and sharing it with your deck before its first use. I know it might sound unusual, but your new deck will be your trusted friend, and simple rituals like these will help to strengthen that bond.

Similarly, you may wish to do divination with a pendulum or dowsing rods. You may even wish to charge them with the power of the goddess by wrapping them up in natural fabric overnight with power crystals or herbs for divination between uses. Sometimes I even use cards or my pendulum when I want to ask a question of a specific foremother, goddess, loa, or orisha. The possibilities are absolutely endless and limited only by your imagination.

2

OSHÚN, THE RIVER OF BEAUTY AND LOVE

Beauty, love, money, fertility, honey, gold—the orisha Oshún represents all the good things in life. She embodies the sweet things that are as old as time. She is called by many names in many, many places—Osun in Nigeria, Oxum in Brazil, Oshún in Cuba—and each incarnation is equally regal, albeit slightly different. Her worship is international and truly legendary.

In a very generalized sense, all women are seen to be Oshún's daughters, part of a direct lineage from this divine mother. But then most specifically in the religion she is said to claim certain ones as Omo Oshún, or having the head of Oshún. Discovering this can be determined by divination and ceremony with multiple babalawos, or priests.

My personal journey to this powerful goddess Oshún was a winding one, just like the river itself. Like many women of color, I was attracted to this quintessence of beauty. I was captivated by Oshún's aura, her energy, and her Ashe. I read all I could find. I talked to everyone who might know her true path. I studied everyone associated with her in ritual, and out. I had a few false starts, as many people do on the path, but when I finally had the divination to determine who owns my head in my spiritual house,

Oshún came through loud and proud. It is a true honor to be associated with this orisha who reminds me daily of the joy and beauty to be found in life. Her love and blessings continue to be a guiding force in all that I do.

The Myth and the Reality of Oshún

In the tradition of La Regla Lucumi, one of the ways spiritual lessons are taught is through *patakis,* or sacred stories. They are told as part of one's divinations, or just when elders feel that others in the religion need to hear them. There is simultaneously only one right way to tell these tales, and a million right ways to tell them. Such is the nature of the religion, which is richly based in oral history and legend that leaves itself open to personal interpretation. There are fortunately elaborate stories to illustrate almost every principle and message the orisha Oshún has set out to teach us. One of the most popular reminds us just how strong she is, and shows that strength is not always defined just in physical terms. The strength and power of this warrior orisha lie not only in her physical strength, but in her intelligence and boundless powers of persuasion. The Ashe (sacred energy) of Oshún is that of the sweet river. It is both magnetic and irresistible. The following well-known story tells of how in many situations she is stronger, and more successful, than any of the other orishas.

It came to be, many years ago, that a group of very powerful witches hiding in the woods had the intent to take over the world. These were menstruating females, whose moon time had increased their strength and ability. This made them virtually unstoppable. The orishas all gathered and discussed how to best put an end to the witches' plans. First the orisha Ogun, in charge of war and iron, was sent to discourage them. The witches, however, were too powerful, and despite his massive size and battle skills, he was unsuccessful. Many of the other orishas tried too, but they had no luck. Finally, Oshún took charge. She mesmerized the witches with her sensual dances and sweet power. They immediately fell in love and began to follow her. She then took on an aspect as queen of witches, and they are still following her today. Oshún, as illustrated, has the ability to command and control almost any situation.

One area that is always of interest to Oshún is love and relationships. There are stories of her being romantically involved with other orishas, such as Chango, Orula, Ogun, Inle, and others. Her interactions with her suitors are legendary, and one story explains this part of her history beautifully.

Long ago, Oshún lived in her mother Yemaya's house. Each day she would go deep into the woods and dance and sing. Even far removed from people, she still attracted them with her sheer sensual power and magnetism. Every time a hungry suitor got close enough to speak to her and ask her to marry him, she would turn her back and dance away. Soon, scores of admirers followed her all day and all night. They would even appear at her mother's house, looking for attention. Day after day, more and more appeared. They began to intrude on the space, trampling the garden, ruining the crops, and disturbing the household. Finally, Oshún's mother could stand it no more, and she burst from the house yelling, "Stop it! This is unacceptable. I know my daughter is captivating, but this must come to an end."

Oshún's mother decided to devise a clever contest. She told the desperate crowd, "All of you wish to have my daughter as your wife, but how can you do that if none of you even know her name? The one who learns her name will have my permission to truly be with her." The potential lovers did everything in their power to discover her secret name. They asked everyone in the village, to no avail.

One of the suitors was Orunmila, the orisha of divination. Again and again he tried to use his psychic powers to learn her name but had no luck. In the end, he turned to his friend Eleggua to help him learn the secret. Eleggua is an orisha known for his ability to open doors, find lost things, and create clever solutions to any problem. He accepted the challenge to find the name of the most beautiful woman in the land.

Eleggua tried every trick he knew to learn the name. First he disguised himself as a young child and played beneath Oshún's window, hoping to hear someone inside speak her name. When that tactic was unsuccessful, he turned himself into an old homeless man and slept all night on her doorstep, all in the hopes of learning her name. He did this for many nights. Just when he was about to give up hope, he heard a large crash and yelling coming from the house. He looked inside to find the two women yelling. Oshún had been practicing a new dance move, and one of her turns had broken a soup pot. Her mother screamed, "Oshún! Be careful." Eleggua quickly went back to his friend with this knowledge.

Orunmila was so excited to hear the results. "Tell me, tell me!" He pleaded.

Eleggua described the hardships he had undergone to learn the name. "I had to be a child and run around under their window all day, and then I had to be an old beggar and sleep on their uncomfortable doorstep for many nights," Eleggua said.

"Please, please, please I must know," Orunmila responded. He was almost begging.

Finally, Eleggua said her name. Orunmila ran to Oshún's house and told her mother the secret name. Shortly after, they were married. It is said that for a great number of years they were happy together.

Come See the River

In the African diasporic religions, Oshún is described as the Ashe of the river. It is here that her truly sacred energy resides. A river is a liminal place, the sacred site of in-between where magick is made. It is a place of both earth and water. Here is a divine crossroads of spiritual energy. It is fertile with potential and possibility. This is the location where people leave offerings to Oshún, and also where her holy ceremonies are held.

Oshún's river water is a divine vehicle of healing. It is this water that makes all of life possible. She is vital to creation in this world and the next. This is true in all the religions where she is honored, from Ifa to

Lucumi to Candomble. It is easy to see how newcomers to the tradition have a hard time understanding this orisha; she has the divine power to both bless and birth. Her sweet rivers represent the amniotic fluid of the entire world. Some say she was given this power of water from Yemaya, who is sometimes seen as her mother, or alternatively her sister.

The Many Faces of Oshún

As I have mentioned, Oshún is an orisha that manifests in many different traditions. Even within Santeria she has many paths, or different incarnations, where she shows herself beautifully. There is a path where she is seen as an old woman who sits at the bottom of the river knitting and complaining; there is one where she is always crying and hoping things were different; there is one where she is always laughing and seeing the truth in life (some say when she is laughing you should watch out). Some paths are aligned with the orisha Chango, lord of fire; some are connected to Ogun, the orisha of smiths and war; and one is even seen as revolutionary and has a special connection to the orisha Ochosi, who wears his ceremonial arrow on her crown. There are many more. Each one delightfully mimics the exact character of Oshún's children. Through proper initiation and divination, the particular path that is guiding you will be revealed.

Oshún in Other Aspects

Traditionally, Oshún is represented visually with the Catholic image of Nuestra Senora de la Caridad del Cobre, or the Virgin Mary. This image has been used for centuries both because of its availability and because for many years these practices were performed in secret. Using a Catholic image allowed practitioners to carry out their religion without being exposed to prejudice and possible persecution.

Many scholars theorize this particular image was used for Oshún because she is surrounded by water and a boat. Others think that it is because of Oshún's great charity and compassion that she is associated with *la caridad,* which means "charity" in Spanish.

The boat at the feet of Nuestra Senora de la Caridad del Cobre has now taken on its own mythology. Inside the boat are three men all named Juan. It is said that in the 1600s a pair of brothers (one named Juan) and a young slave named Juan were in a boat off the shores of Cuba during a severe storm at sea when they found a statue of Nuestra Senora de la Caridad del Cobre. They credited her for their survival, and she eventually became the patron saint of Cuba.

Over 13 percent of Cuba's population of eleven million currently practice La Regla Lucumi. There have long been rumors of statues of Nuestra Senora de la Caridad del Cobre being dressed in military fatigues in honor of former president Fidel Castro. You can easily see again how she takes on a warrior character in this manifestation. She is called on to help an individual through stormy times, both in the visible and invisible world.

The boat is also said to help devotees navigate stormy times, too. Some devotees even craft small boats on which to float their offerings and desires out onto the river for her.

I remember one time my friend's five-year-old daughter came to visit me. She saw one of my statues of Nuestra Senora de la Caridad del Cobre high up on a shelf. Her eyes grew wide. "It's a princess," she said. It was in that moment when I truly understood Oshún's universal appeal. Oshún's regal beauty shines brighter than that of Cinderella, Rapunzel, Sleeping Beauty, Tiana, and the rest, no matter what your age.

Very often, modern depictions of Oshún show her with her ritual fan and ritual bell. The fan is said to help cool your head, so you will be able to stay calm and focused in all situations. Her bells are said to ring out and help devotees clearly hear the truth.

In 2015, Pope Francis made a visit to Cuba to see Oshún in all her regal glory. This made him the third pope in a row to grace the island. One major difference, however, is this time the Pope went to see the patron of the place, Nuestra Senora de la Caridad del Cobre. Many in Cuba and throughout the world see this aspect of the Virgin Mary as associated with the Santeria orisha Oshún, and the Pope's sermon during mass at Basílica de Nuestra Señora del Cobre indeed spoke of Mary. Some devotees see this as a subtle nod to Santeria, while others viewed it as yet another attempt by the Church to appropriate and coopt elements of the religion.

Probably the most famous current public appearance of Oshún is via music icon Beyoncé. Celebrities and Santeria often come together. For years, there have been unconfirmed rumors of performers like J-Lo, Carlos Santana, Celia Cruz, and even Beyoncé being initiated in the tradition. Beyoncé, known as Queen Bey to those who know and love her, has begun to incorporate hints of the orisha in her stage shows and videos in recent years. This has introduced Oshún to a whole new audience, in a whole new context. After her 2017 Grammy performance, which gave a covert nod to Oshún, Beyoncé was called everything from a demon to a goddess to a crazy person. One article even cautioned against her being considered a "mammy," and everything that stereotype holds. Suddenly there were hundreds of young women of color who newly embraced this Golden Goddess–like image. However, there were also staunch traditionalists who disagreed with her medium, if not her message.

Popular music has given a lot of attention to this orisha lately, and I would be failing if I did not mention two groups in connection with Oshún. The first is Ibeyi, a French duo comprised of twins Lisa-Kaindé and Naomi Diaz. The Diaz sisters even appeared in Beyoncé's video "Lemonade," which was full of Oshún sacred symbolism. Ibeyi's most widely known song, "River," is a lyrical tribute to Oshún. In it they sing ritual chants in Yoruba for the goddess. In many ways, it is almost as if new generations of women are embracing the Oshún energy, and this is most definitely true for the New York City–based duo Niambi Sala and Thandiwe. Together, these two are the musical group Oshún. Their empowering mission is to educate and celebrate. These women have become she-roes to younger generations, and I'm excited to see what both pairs of performers do moving forward.

Dancing Queen

In addition to being in charge of love, beauty, fertility, and sensuality, Oshún is the orisha of dance. Her ritual dances are coquettish and seductive. Special costumes are made for the dancers in ceremony, which are traditionally in Oshún's ritual colors of yellow and gold.

There are many stories featuring Oshún's adventures at the river. In the Afro-Cuban tradition of La Regla Lucumi, the ritual dances done for this orisha also help to illustrate these sacred teaching stories. This is because by immersing oneself in all the elements of the religion, an individual can hope to gain greater understanding. One of the traditional movements included in the Oshún dance mimics a ritual story where she is bathing herself in the river. Some of the hand movements mime lifting water high up and over the body, cleansing and blessing oneself. There are other traditional movements where her hands are lifted upward in a gesture of joy and ecstasy. Very often during the dance, she uses her fan to both call and cast out energy with artful movements. She can also use her mirror, mimicked by her hand, to admire herself, and also to see behind her during the dance. These beautifully illustrate aspects of her character though the graceful medium of dance.

When we are speaking of spirituality, there is no substitute for doing—so if you have a chance to learn the orisha dances for yourself, I highly recommend it. Most communities with large Afro-Latinx populations have places that offer these types of classes. Please check out your local cultural organizations and resources to connect. Devotees spend years, if not decades, carefully perfecting the intricate movements. The feeling of the motions through your body is like nothing else. They allow you to get out of your own head and back in your body. Dance, and more specifically repetitive movement, is key to accessing the higher realms.

The Familiar Oshún

A variety of sacred animals are connected to Oshún. In Nigeria, Osun is seen as the crocodile, the hippo, and the vulture. Other parts of the world see Oshún as a sacred peacock in all its colorful glory. This is certainly true in the tradition of La Regla Lucumi, where Oshún is frequently given ritual fans made of peacock plumes. In some houses she is even represented with the Ashe of the buzzard, which is said to embody her power to protect against all evil.

There is one particular ritual story that speaks of her specific connection to the vulture and elevating to her rightful place as queen.

It is said that when Olofi created the earth and its inhabitants, he would communicate with them through the ceiba tree. The ceiba tree holds a special significance in the religion, and even my late santo godmother took great pains to make sure she had one in her yard. At this time in our story, Olofi provided everything for his newly formed creations. Instead of being grateful, and preparing for the future, the individuals under his care became lazy and complacent. This disappointed Olofi, and he decided to stop helping people altogether. Because they were used to having everything given to them, they had not had the foresight to plant any crops or cultivate any food. Very soon a severe famine spread through the land. It was then that the orisha Oshún decided to take action.

Oshún transformed herself into a vulture and flew straight up into the sky to find Olofi. She brought him food, for he had been starving too. Olofi was very grateful, and also deeply moved by Oshún's kindness and compassion. He asked what in the world he could do to repay her for her generosity and kindness. Oshún thought for a long time and then finally answered him. Oshún wanted to help all the others who were hungry and in need, so she asked Olofi for the food to do this. Olofi explained that he could not help, but he did know someone who could.

He told her that on the way back down to earth she would pass through the lands of the farmer orisha Oko. Oko was the one who would be able to help her. Oshún did indeed find Oko and his farm on her way back down to earth. Oko was surrounded by his harvest, and he gave Oshún all the food she wanted to take. She returned to earth and fed the people. They crowned her queen, and she has been queen ever since.

Another ritual story of Oshún talks about her fertility, one of her greatest gifts. However, it is known that she does not participate in the day-to-day raising of her children; that task is given to her mother, Yemaya. This story explains this, saying Oshún's children were taken from her and brought to another land. Some believe that land was Cuba. Obviously distraught, it is said she searched the world over for them until she found them there. She then followed to the New World to be with them and become the patron deity of the island nation. In these stories we can see how Oshún is always motivated by great love and compassion

Oshún Herbs and Offerings

Oshún, like all the orishas, is honored with her own specific combination of herbs, spices, and flowers. The herbs and offerings serve as a vessel for the Ashe of the orisha to travel through. Botanicals like these can be used in magickal candle dressings, baths, floor washes, gris-gris, sprinkling powders, and more. A partial list for Oshún includes the following:

- Allspice
- Anise
- Basil
- Catnip
- Chamomile
- Cinnamon
- Clover
- Cloves
- Copal
- Daisies
- Dill
- Elderflower
- Female ferns
- Galangal
- Gardenia
- Ginger
- Ginseng
- Heliotrope
- Honeysuckle
- Hyssop
- Jasmine
- Lavender
- Lemongrass
- Lotus

- Marigolds
- Marjoram
- Myrtle
- Nutmeg
- Orange blossoms
- Orchids
- Orris root
- Parsley
- Peaches
- Peppermint
- Primrose
- Rosemary
- Roses
- Sesame seed
- Sweet peas
- Sunflowers
- Tangerines
- Tonka beans
- Vanilla

A few years back, I had the opportunity to create a sacred garden for Oshún at the Brushwood Folklore Center in Sherman, New York. Located on Pagan-owned land, the locale has long been a site for festivals, events, and celebrations. It was almost as if the site was divinely prepared for us ahead of time. Four trees had formed a beautiful boundary, a little oasis in the forest. We cleaned, weeded, and spiritually blessed the space. Next we filled it with Oshún's sacred plants—lavender, rosemary, sunflowers, roses, and more. We also offered crystals like amber and citrine, riverbed shells, golden rocks, and peacock feathers. It has become an ever-evolving sacred space where people can come and connect to the divine Ashe of Oshún, and I'm hoping the garden will continue to grow and thrive over time. Please think about visiting it if you have the chance.

In Nigeria, the sacred shrines for Osun are directly in nature. They are manifestations of spirit where people can honor and give tribute to the orisha. The Osun river runs through the country. However, the most famous site is the Osun-Osogbo Sacred Grove in Osogbo, Osun State, Nigeria, northwest of Lagos. This sacred forest is protected as a UNESCO World Heritage site. The word *oshogbo* roughly breaks down to Oshún and Ogbo, which means "Osun's stage." This place literally is a sacred stage for the goddess. Traditionally, sacred groves like this one were established outside towns and villages. Unfortunately, the modern world has encroached on many of these areas, and this is one of the few still in existence. Here the religion is referred to as Ifa. These sacred shrines in nature take precedence over any indoor or humanmade creation.

One way to honor Oshún before you take the necessary steps towards initiation is to create her ritual recipes. These can be made for her feast day, September 8, or anytime you wish to give her tribute. There are many sacred stories that speak of this orisha and food. The most famous tells of the time she was poisoned by one of her many jealous rivals. Because of this, Oshún and her children are often mistrustful and picky about food. If you are using or offering honey at any time, tradition dictates that it always be tasted first.

It is also worthy of mentioning here that once someone has become "seated" as a santero or santera (priest or priestess) in the Lucumi faith, they are often unable to eat that orisha's sacred foods, as these become taboo. One time, many years ago, my spiritual house was hosting our annual Oshún feast and we had a problem. The extensive menu featured xin-xin/ochin-ochin (a traditional dish for Oshún made with shrimp and eggs), orange cake with honey, and other treasures. When two santeras and one santero dedicated to Oshún showed up unexpectedly, I scrambled to find extra food for them to eat. Expect the unexpected, I always say, as these are all things to be mindful of as you navigate these complex waters known as the Ashe of Oshún. In the meantime, until one continues with initiation in the tradition, the following recipes can be used for honoring and feasts.

OSHÚN'S BUTTERNUT SQUASH SOUP

Oshún is customarily offered pumpkins, squash, and gourds. These hearken back to her powers of fertility and abundance. Her offerings are most often presented in ritual gourds to represent the primal womb of creation.

Ingredients

- 2 tablespoons butter
- ½ Vidalia onion, chopped
- 3 cups butternut squash, peeled and cubed
- 2 cups chicken broth
- ½ cup applesauce
- ¼ teaspoon ground sage
- ½ teaspoon parsley
- ½ teaspoon onion powder
- Pinch each of cinnamon, nutmeg, and ginger
- ¼ cup cream
- Salt and pepper to taste
- Sunflower seeds
- Pumpkin seeds
- Fresh sage

Melt butter in saucepan over low heat. Place onion in pan and simmer until it begins to lose its color. In a separate pan, place the butternut squash and add just enough water to cover. Bring the squash to a boil and cook until tender. Drain the squash, mash it, and add it to the pan with onion. Add chicken broth, applesauce, sage, parsley, onion powder, cinnamon, nutmeg, and ginger, and mix thoroughly. Simmer soup over low heat for 10 minutes, stirring occasionally. Remove from heat, stir in cream, and add salt and pepper to taste. Serve in a pumpkin bowl topped with sunflower and pumpkin seeds and a sprig of fresh sage. Serves 4 to 6. ■

OSHÚN'S MANGO SALSA FOR LOVE

This is one of my favorite summer recipes to prepare for this orisha. It contains two of her ritual fruits, orange and mango, which combine artfully with traditional salsa ingredients to make a wonderful creation.

Ingredients

- 2 ripe mangoes, pitted, peeled, and diced
- 6 ripe plum tomatoes, chopped and seeded
- 1 red onion, diced
- 1 yellow pepper, seeded and chopped
- 2 cloves garlic, minced
- 3 tablespoons orange juice
- ¼ cup cilantro, chopped
- ¼ cup parsley, chopped
- ½ teaspoon salt
- 1 teaspoon onion powder
- 1 teaspoon chili powder
- Pinch of cinnamon
- 1 tablespoon apple cider vinegar
- 2 tablespoons hot sauce (more or less to taste)

Mix mangoes, tomatoes, onion, pepper, and garlic in a large glass or ceramic bowl. Add remaining ingredients and stir clockwise to combine.

Cover and refrigerate the mixture for at least 2 hours. Serve with chips, crackers, veggies, or whatever tickles you like Oshún does! Makes approximately 2 cups. ■

OSHÚN FROZEN BELLINI

Many of the orishas are known to enjoy liquor and spirits as an offering. Oshún is fond of champagne and/or prosecco. This recipe combines those with two other things she loves—white peaches and mango.

Ingredients

- 2 cups frozen white peach slices
- 1 cup mango nectar
- 2 pinches of cinnamon
- 1 bottle chilled champagne or prosecco
- 6 sprigs of peppermint, for garnish

Combine peaches, mango nectar, and cinnamon in a blender and pulse until combined. Fill six champagne flutes half-full with the mixture. Top off each glass with chilled champagne or prosecco and garnish with peppermint sprigs, edible flowers, cinnamon sticks, or additional slices of mango or peach. ■

OSHÚN FRUIT SALAD

A variety of fruits are said to be sacred offerings for Oshún. It is almost as if these symbols of nature's fertility show us the sensuality and fertility of Oshún as well. This recipe blends some of her traditional offerings into a delightful medley of flavors that has been described by those I've served it to as "sex in a bowl."

Ingredients

- 3 peaches, peeled and sliced
- 2 mangoes, peeled and diced
- ½ cup orange juice
- 1 ounce peach schnapps (optional)

- ½ teaspoon orange zest
- ¼ teaspoon cinnamon
- ¼ teaspoon nutmeg
- Pinch of cloves

Combine fruit in a large ceramic or glass bowl. Pour the orange juice and schnapps (if using) into a measuring cup. Add the orange zest and spices. Stir well in a clockwise motion to combine. Pour the juice mixture over the fruit and mix well. Chill for at least 2 hours. Serve cold. ■

OSHÚN RITUAL BATH FOR BLESSINGS AND JOY

After divination, ritual baths are probably the most popular solution for people who are facing life challenges. This bath is designed to surround you with the Ashe of Oshún. In La Regla Lucumi, much importance is placed on taking ritual baths. These are created to cleanse and bless the body. Many effective premade bath formulas are available, but you can also try making your own.

Ingredients

- ½ gallon spring water
- 1 cup river water
- 3 drops rose absolute or 1 cup rose water
- 3 drops sunflower oil
- 3 drops cinnamon oil
- 3 drops orange blossom oil

Combine all ingredients in a large white bowl and stir clockwise with a wooden spoon.

Reserve a small amount which you will take to the nearest river after the bath is done, and leave it as an offering along with five coins. These can be coins in any denomination, but it is best to use things like nickels or quarters, as they align with Oshún's sacred number, 5.

When you are ready to take the ritual bath, pour the mixture into the bath or a large tub. Soak in the magickal water for 10 minutes. When you are done, dispose of the water down the drain or pour it out onto the earth.

Note: This formula can also be used as a floor wash to clean your home or temple. ■

OSHÚN PROSPERITY OIL

Worshipers of African traditional religions, from Benin to Bahia, all use magickal oils. This particular one is crafted for Oshún. Like most deities and most people, Oshún has a good side and a not-so-good side. She is an orisha of money, fertility, and bounty. Part of the reason she is given dominion over these areas is because she has struggled with them herself. There are various stories to illustrate this point.

The following oil uses herbs and a special money cowrie shell to help attract prosperity. Some historians believe the cowrie shell was one of the first systems of money used. The money cowrie mentioned here is a cowrie shell which has been split across the top to make it see-through on both sides.

Oshún's ritual days are Tuesday and Saturday, so this oil is best prepared during these days.

Ingredients

- 1 ounce sweet almond oil
- 5 drops amber oil
- 5 drops orange oil
- 5 drops sunflower oil
- 1 money cowrie shell
- Pinch of dried cinquefoil (five-finger grass)
- Pinch of dried patchouli

Assemble all ingredients on your ritual table or altar. Add the oils to the large-mouth mason jar. Next add the cowrie shell, cinquefoil, and patchouli. Shake well as you focus on money and abundance coming to you. Place the oil in an undisturbed place outside or on your windowsill and leave it there for 24 hours. This will allow the rays of the sun and the moon to bless and consecrate it. After this, it is ready to use.

Wear Oshún Prosperity Oil when you go on a job interview, ask for a loan or a raise, or need to attune yourself to financial success. ■

OSHÚN HONEY JAR

Undoubtedly, the most popular working for Oshún is the honey jar. There are hundreds of practitioners, if not thousands, who are doing these spells for their clients. Unfortunately, many are not properly trained in the religion, and their results can be questionable at best and disastrous at worst. You can, however, make your own honey jar—not to trap a man or get a million dollars, but to honor this divine orisha and give tribute to her life-sustaining energy.

Ingredients

- 1 jar organic honey with comb in (orange blossom if possible)
- 5 drops ginger oil
- 5 drops orange oil
- 1 whole nutmeg
- 5 cinnamon sticks
- Rose water
- Small yellow candle

Gather all ingredients on your working altar or shrine. Begin by tasting the honey with your index finger. This is to show Oshún that it is safe. Next, add the essential oils and nutmeg. Stir the mixture gently clockwise with each of the cinnamon sticks; then add them to the jar. (You may need to pour out some honey to make room.) Cover the jar. Pour a small amount of rose water in the bottom of a candle holder and place a yellow candle in it. Position the candle in front of your honey jar. Light it. As it burns, you may want to offer some ritual drumming or chants for Oshún. When the candle has burned down, your honey is ready for use. Keep it in a sacred place in your home.

When you are done with the honey, feel free to dispose of it at the river, along with five oranges as an offering. ■

OSHÚN CANDLE

If you travel to your local botanica (spiritual supply store), you will see that Oshún is one of the most popular candles sold at the place. People love to honor this orisha of love in good times and bad. You can buy candles that feature Nuestra Senora de la Caridad del Cobre, or a more African-based image of Oshún, with copper skin, a mirror, and sunflowers. If neither of these are available, you could use a simple yellow or gold candle.

You can light a candle like this for Oshún's feast day on September 8, or whenever you want to honor her presence in your life.

Ingredients

- Oshún 7-day candle
- 3 drops jasmine oil
- 3 drops ylang-ylang oil
- 5 drops primrose oil
- 5 drops sunflower oil

Assemble all ingredients on your ritual table or a clean, undisturbed space. Light the candle. After it has been burning for 15 to 30 minutes, add the oils. This allows the oils to mix completely with the wax. Do your best to focus all your energy and attention on the candle as it burns. Obviously, never leave a burning candle unattended. If needs must, you can extinguish the candle and relight it again later until it has burned out. Burn the candle as often as possible until the wax has disappeared. ■

SETTING A TABLE FOR OSHÚN

One of the things people do on the feast day of Oshún, September 8, is set a ritual table for her. This is similar to an altar or shrine. Here you can incorporate many of the things in this chapter to create a sacred space.

Ingredients

- Image for Oshún
- Water for Oshún
- Candle for Oshún
- Incense for Oshún
- Piece of amber or river sand
- Food offering for Oshún
- Flowers
- Any additional offerings you'd like to include

Ready the space for the table. Start your creation by finding an image to represent this orisha. It could be a picture or statue of Nuestra Senora de la Caridad del Cobre, or one of the more African images of this orisha. You could even use her sacred symbol, called a *ponto*, which is often sewn onto cloth and then used to cover drums and other ritual items. The ponto for Oshún usually incorporates hearts and stars, showing her as a guiding force of love in the universe. It is best to also include an item from each of the elements: water, fire, air, and earth.

- To represent the water, use river water. Place this in a glass or ceramic container and put it on the ritual table. If you like, you can add a small amount of rose water or Florida Water, which are also known to please her. Oshún is the Ashe of the river, so wherever you have river water she is present.
- The element of fire is most often present in the form of a candle. This can be a simple yellow candle, or a fully consecrated one like has been described. Because her sacred number is 5, some people like to use five small taper or votive candles to honor her.
- A simple Oshún incense to represent the element of air can be made by placing some of her ritual herbs on a piece of charcoal and burning them. Please be careful when selecting your herbs, however, as some—like cinnamon—can be irritating when burned. You can also purchase ready-made incense specifically for this orisha.
- Some devotees of Oshún use amber to represent the element of earth on her ritual table. Amber is created from plant resin that has hardened over centuries. Like Oshún herself, it has stood the test of time to become stronger and sweeter. Dirt or sand that has been gathered from the riverside are also acceptable to use here. These will help to ground and center your creation.

The next thing to include when setting your ritual table is food. You can make any of the sacred recipes in this chapter, or you can simply include some of her favorite fruits and vegetables. These include, but are not limited to, pumpkins, squash, cantaloupes, mangoes, plantains, and oranges.

Oshún represents beauty in all forms, and she is particularly fond of flowers. Please be sure to include a bouquet of her favorite blooms—sunflowers, yellow roses, and marigolds are great options.Make sure to feature some of her other favorite offerings too, like a mirror, jewelry, fishhooks, a fan, gold and/or money, and honey that you have tasted first. The mirror and the jewelry are said to represent her vanity, which is the same reason she is associated with the peacock.

After all these components have been laid out, use the space to meditate and give tribute to Oshún. As always, be sure to check with your godparents in the tradition for personalized guidance and direction. ■

Oshún can bless her children with joy, happiness, gold, healing, and much more. She shows us her power and strength as a warrior queen who can triumph in any situation. Her dancing feet gracefully touch down in all corners of the globe: Nigeria, Cuba, Brazil, the United States, and elsewhere. It is as if her glory knows no bounds. Consequently, Oshún's different paths are plentiful: she can manifest with a machete or drums, a quail or vulture, a song and a dance, a laugh or a fight—myriad ways. She is a queen worthy of center stage at the Grammys, and an audience with the Pope. Oshún is love—love for ourselves, our families, our heritage, our community. She shows us how this love is a great strength that allows us to succeed against all odds.

3

YEMAYA, THE OCEAN OF MOTHERLY LOVE

There is a sacred power, a force of nature, that rolls on the waves and rides the high seas. Her name is Yemaya. Present in many different religions, she goes by many names—Yemayá, Iemanja, Janaína, and Yemonja. Hers is a path of sacred tradition, fluidity, and innovation. In the tradition of La Regla Lucumi, she is known as an orisha, one of the divine forces that rule the universe. Many hear her sacred song of maternal love, kindness, and blessing.

Yemaya is customarily celebrated on her feast day of September 7, which coincides with the Catholic day for Diosa del Mar, the Lady of the Sea. In this representation, shimmering stars fall from her hands as she rises gracefully above the cresting ocean waves. In Brazil, celebrations for her Candomble avatar Iemanja occur on December 31 and are combined with the New Year's Eve festivities to make quite a show. Cakes, flowers, and rafts are floated out to sea to celebrate this orisha. It is truly a sight to see. Some spiritual houses associate Yemaya with Our Lady of Candelaria and thus use the feast day of February 2, while some people associate her with Mother's Day. In Havana, she is sometimes depicted as La Virgen de Regla, who is also the patron saint of the bay of Havana.

In many houses, Yemaya has a counterpart or companion named Olokun. Olokun represents the depths of the ocean, while Yemaya is said to own the foaming waves of the sea.

Newcomers to African traditional religion often feel a connection to this orisha. In her they can recognize an ancient and powerful mother, both nurturing and protecting. As with most orishas, there are several paths, or *caminos,* of this divinity. One path of Yemaya is the sister of Oshún, who lives and plays with her in the river. Another path is an "ocean of blood" who cares for all the shipwreck victims. Yet another avatar oversees all the buried treasure that lies at the bottom of the ocean. There is a common belief that Yemaya is always a gentle mother. But don't cross her—or cause harm to her children—or you will see the full depths of the anger that this orisha is capable of unleashing.

There are many ritual stories, or *patakis,* for Yemaya that illustrate these different paths. One story tells of her temporarily changing herself into the river in order to flee an angry mate and escape back to the ocean.

Another tells of the relationship between Yemaya and her sister Oshún. It is said that when Oshún was born, she had a white dress. White clothes are customary for those in all the orisha-based faiths. One of the characteristics of this orisha is that she is renowned for her cleanliness and takes great pride in her impeccable appearance. Oshún spent much time tending to her flowing hair, and admiring her beauty in the mirror, or in the river when no mirror was available. A queen among queens, she ruled over her subjects with beauty and kindness. After a time, a violent war erupted in the land, and Oshún was forced to flee her beloved kingdom.

It was not long before Oshún was destitute. She was forced to sell her fine jewelry to survive. She only had one dress, and it was white. She had no choice but to wash it in the river, and it began to yellow. Her days and nights were filled with extreme sadness and anxiety. Due to all this worrying her hair began to fall out. Each day she cried at the river, longing for all she had lost.

Fortunately, her cries did not go unanswered. At the end of the river, where it meets the sea, was Oshún's sister, Yemaya. Yemaya longed to help Oshún in her time of need. She reminded her that despite everything she was still a queen. She saw Oshún's yellow dress and proclaimed it would now be gold, and all the gold in the land would belong to Oshún as well. This was along with all the coral from the sea. Riches and finery would soon be hers again. Yemaya also noticed what had happened to Oshún's lovely hair. She immediately cut off half of her hair and fashioned a wig for Oshún to wear until her own tresses had the chance to grow back even stronger. The love between these sisters is truly legendary, and they will always do their best to support one another.

Another pataki describes Yemaya's complicated relationship with the orisha Inlé. Yemaya has had many relationships in her time, and a particularly interesting one was with her lover Inlé, whom she taught the secret art of divination. Despite Yemaya sharing her talents with Inlé, in the end he abandoned her. Filled with rage, she cut out his tongue so he would not be able to share with anyone else the knowledge he had gained from her. She quickly regretted her decision, but the deed had already been done. From that time forward, Inlé was only able to speak to others through Yemaya's voice. As I have mentioned, there are variations in Yemaya's worship across houses, and definitely across nations too. Among the Yoruba people of the Ifa faith she is called Yemoja, which is said to mean Mother of Fish. Here she is viewed as an ancient orisha, existing almost since the beginning of time. She is seen to have birthed all forms of creation. She is seen to be a protector of all women and children, and all their concerns. Legend tells us that when enslaved Africans were taken from their homeland and forcibly placed on ships, many had never seen the full expanse of the ocean before, and believed that it would swallow them up. These individuals prayed to Yemaya to save their lives. When they finally reached land, they kissed the ground and said, "Oh my Yemaya, thank you." This story may have evolved in response to the chant for Yemaya in Yoruba, "Omio Yemoja," which loosely translates to "water of Yemoja." You may wish to use it in conjunction with your offerings or prayers.

The number 7 is frequently connected to this orisha. She is said to have seven paths or avatars, and offerings to her are customarily left in multiples of seven. Some, however, count many more paths, each one with its own unique character. I remember once I was with a friend who is a santera (Santeria priestess) dedicated to Yemaya, and we were both wearing our *elekes*, or ritual necklaces for the orisha. Someone came up to us and remarked that the necklace she had for Yemaya was very dainty, with dark and light blues and tiny silver fishes, while the one I had was much darker, containing garnet beads interspersed with the traditional dark blue. They wondered why this was. I explained that the path my friend was dedicated to was much gentler than the one followed by my spiritual house. They took a small step back when I explained that the garnet beads in my strand represented blood. Although this is a humorous story, it again illustrates the value of initiation and working with a teacher. My friend had been given the proper Yemaya for her to worship, as was I; these, however, were very different energies. Luckily, we knew enough to seek proper guidance and find out what was right for us.

Yemaya in Art and Music

Yemaya is prevalent in art and music dedicated to the orisha. In Cuba she was even honored with a stamp to commemorate the anniversary of the Conjunto Folklórico Nacional de Cuba, a national arts collective that performs orisha dances. In her ritual dances her skirts twirl like the breaking of the waves with grace and precision. If you have the opportunity to attend an orisha dance workshop, I highly recommend it—not as a substitute for initiation, but as a creative compliment to your practices. One of the most popular Cuban singers of all time was Celia Cruz. She is in part famous for a song dedicated to Yemaya. Born in 1925 in Havana, Cruz went on to win three Grammy Awards and four Latin Grammys, had twenty-three gold records, and received a Lifetime Achievement

Award from the Smithsonian Institution. While it is hotly debated in the community whether or not she was a devotee of Santeria, she often sang songs for the orisha. She began singing songs like "Canto a Yemaya" in the 1950s and continued throughout her life until she passed away in 2003.

Songs for Yemaya have also been recorded by the Afro-Cuban artist Lazaro Ros, as well as Louie Vega and Fernando Hernandez with the Inés Sotomayor Group, which was released in 1998 as part of the Smithsonian Folkways recordings.

One of the most well-known traditional art pieces depicting this orisha is the MaestraPeace Mural in San Francisco's Mission District, created in 1994. The piece, painted on two sides of the Women's Building, stands over five stories high and was created by seven different muralists. One particular artist, Juana Alicia, chose to depict a stunning representation of Yemaya. Here she shows the powerful female majesty of this orisha, who stands with contemporary and ancient women against the evils of inequality and male dominance.

There are several other contemporary women artists who have chosen to honor Yemaya in their work. I am particularly fond of the paintings of Yasmin Hernandez. Her 2003 "Yemaya y Ochun" was commissioned by *El Diario/La Prensa* for their Women's Month Distinguished Latinas Celebration. It shows the two divine ladies holding hands through waters and across worlds.

Herbs and Fruits for Yemaya

Following are some of the most common botanicals used to honor Yemaya, but the list is by no means exhaustive, and you may want to supplement your offerings with ready-made preparations from your local botanica or spiritual supply store. There you will find oils, baths, perfumes, colognes, floor washes, and more specific to the orisha.

- Allspice
- Amaranth
- Aniseed
- Avocados

- Bananas
- Camphor
- Carnations (white)
- Cilantro
- Coconuts
- Corn
- Eucalyptus
- Gardenia
- Grapes (purple)
- Guinea pepper
- Hyacinths
- Indigo
- Jasmine
- Lemon
- Lemon balm
- Lettuce
- Lotus
- Magnolias
- Mugwort
- Myrrh
- Passion flower
- Peonies
- Poppy seed
- Purple basil
- Sandalwood
- Seaweed
- Spearmint
- Vetiver
- Violet
- Watercress
- Watermelons

Yemaya Workings

As with any orisha, when preparing things for them, both the space and the individual must be physically and ritually clean. This can be done by cleaning yourself with salt or Florida Water, or by any of the other methods described in this book.

FLORIDA WATER

Contrary to the implications of the name, Florida Water isn't simply water from the state of Florida. It is a magickal cologne that has been used for hundreds of years. Personally, I am very fond of some of the commercial preparations, not just because of their scent but because of their spiritual potency. The primary ingredients are lemon, bergamot, and cinnamon in an alcohol base. ■

YEMAYA CANDLE

Use this candle to honor Yemaya and to increase the peace in your home and in yourself. For this working you can use a blue or white candle, or one with an image of Yemaya.

Ingredients

- ½ teaspoon coconut oil
- 7 drops sandalwood oil
- 7 drops jasmine oil
- 7 drops lilac oil
- Blue 7-day candle (for best results, get a pull-out candle in glass)

Gather all items on your working altar or shrine. Combine the oils in a small bowl. Next, rub the oils on the candle from the center upward, and then from the center downward. As Yemaya is connected to the moon, consider lighting your candle on the night of the full moon. Each time you light the candle, focus and meditate on the bounty and love of Yemaya washing over you and every aspect of your life. ■

YEMAYA FLOOR WASH

Magickal floor washes are a simple and easy way to cleanse your home or any other space. The area you are working on should be physically clean. If you are working on an area that is covered by carpet, add the wash to a spray bottle and lightly mist it over the carpet. In any case, be sure to pay special attention to corners and edges, as these are spaces where dirt and negativity tend to collect. When creating a floor wash, use fresh ingredients if at all possible. At the botanicas in New York fresh herbs are delivered on Friday mornings, and most of the community comes out at that time to get their ingredients. This specific formula is designed to create an atmosphere of serenity. It can be especially useful in situations where you desire calm.

Ingredients

- 1 cake cascarilla (powdered eggshell)
- 1 cup sea water
- 1 cup spring water
- 1 teaspoon seaweed
- 7 leaves lemon balm
- 7 leaves spearmint
- 7 drops myrrh oil

Start by grating the cascarilla into a fine powder (it usually comes in the form of a small cake).

Place the cascarilla powder in a bowl and add the waters. Stir to combine. Then add the remaining ingredients and stir. Strain the mixture through a natural cotton cloth into a jar. The wash is now ready to use to clean your floors, windows, and doors. ■

PEACE GRIS-GRIS BAG TO HONOR YEMAYA

This bag contains herbs for tranquility and calm. You may wish to add a charm to the bag as well. In Santeria botanicas, these frequently come with tiny medals of Diosa del Mar (Goddess of the Sea) attached to the front of the bag.

Ingredients

- 2 tablespoons dried shredded coconut
- 1 tablespoon dried basil
- 1 tablespoon dried lavender flowers
- 1 tablespoon sea salt
- 7 drops lemon oil
- 7 drops myrrh oil

Gather all ingredients on your ritual altar or shrine. Add the coconut, basil, lavender, and salt in a small bowl. Mix well, stirring in a counter-clockwise direction. Then add the lemon and myrrh oils and stir again. Pour the mixture into a small, blue natural fiber bag and tie shut. The bag is now ready.

It is customary to carry the bag in your left pocket. You may wish to carry it with you whenever you may be dealing with tumultuous situations, or alternatively you can place it under your pillow at night. When you feel it is no longer needed, dispose of the bag in the ocean. ■

YEMAYA WATERMELON SALAD

Food offerings are some of my favorite things to prepare for the orishas, if you haven't noticed. They simultaneously allow you to nourish yourself and the orisha in a wholesome way. The following recipe combines many of Yemaya's favorite offerings and is delightfully refreshing, like a dip in the ocean on a hot summer day.

Ingredients

- 3 cups watermelon, seeded and cubed
- 1 teaspoon lemon juice
- ½ teaspoon poppy seeds
- ½ cup pineapple, cubed
- 1 teaspoon purple basil, minced

Combine all ingredients in a large bowl. Mix well with a wooden spoon. Chill and serve as an offering to Yemaya. ■

SETTING A TABLE FOR YEMAYA

Each orisha has a ritual number, and Yemaya's is 7. The colors most often associated with her are blue and white. These are all things to bear in mind when creating a ritual space for Yemaya. Remember to always consult with your godparents and teachers before setting up any type of orisha shrine or table. They may have separate or individualized instructions that will be helpful to you.

Begin by making sure you have a separate clean space for your shrine. Many Lucumi devotees craft separate cabinets so their shrines can have equal, but divided, space. At the very least, set up your shrine on a table, and cover it with a natural white cloth when others are present, or when you are not actively honoring it.

Ingredients

- Blue cloth made of natural fabric
- Blue candle
- White carnations or hyacinths
- Food offering (use one of the recipes here, or simply leave an offering of fruits or vegetables)
- Ocean water
- Image or statue for Yemaya (African image, or image of Diosa del Mar, or La Virgin de Regla)
- Seashells
- Small silver mirror or silver fish

Set up the items on top of your blue cloth. Arrange them so that the energy can flow. Put on music or say a ritual prayer for Yemaya. Light your candle. You may leave this table in place until the candle has burned down, or on a more permanent basis as a shrine for Yemaya. If you leave it up permanently, be sure it is covered when not in use. ■

Yemaya allows us to bask in the nurturing care of the mother. She provides divine peace and powerful protection for her followers. She blesses her children with abundance and success. Yemaya sends opportunities to you like waves sent to the shore. Take care to understand and respectfully honor this orisha and she will nurture you in return.

4

OYA, THE POWER OF THE WIND

The wind, the tornado, the hurricane—all of these are the domain of the great and powerful orisha Oya. She is the active embodiment of change. Oya can very often manifest as change in the form of severe weather. She is the lightning strike that hits with insane accuracy.

Civil rights activist Dick Gregory used to speak of the HER-icane, a powerful force of wind that started in Africa, where the roots of mass slavery began, and carried its anger over the ocean, destroying the New World and finally stopping at Canada. This is the kind of energy Oya brings.

Oya's Ashe, or sacred life force, is said to reside in the Niger River, which in the Yoruba language bears her name. And just like the river, she brings opportunity with every twist and turn. Her power is multifaceted and multidimensional. Oya has the power to travel between spaces and worlds, between the living and the dead.

Orishas have complex relationships, just like humans. It is widely accepted in the Ifa and La Regla Lucumi traditions that certain orishas are kept separate. Oya is never honored or called in a ceremony with Oshún or Yemaya, and vice versa. It is known that these ladies do not get along. Similarly, you should keep these orishas separate in your practice, both physically and spiritually. The reasons for these disagreements are illustrated in the sacred tales of the African traditional religions.

Some devotees believe Oya is both the gatekeeper and queen of the dead. She carries her whip and machete, or twin swords, ready to battle all obstacles that stand in her way. She is also known as Yansa, which means Mother of Nine. Oya is thought to have brought nine children into the world, and they are represented by the nine colors in her rainbow skirt. As you might guess, her sacred number is 9, and her colors are either purple or all the colors of the rainbow.

Faces of the Wind

A rainbow skirt isn't the only thing that is said to represent Oya. While most orishas have a single saint representing them on candles and in statuary form, Oya has many. She is equated with St. Teresa of Ávila, Santa Marta and the dragon, and Our Lady of Candelaria. This could be because, at her core, Oya is a shape-shifter. Just like the changing winds that she commands, her form is often flexible and elusive. Many practices illustrate this useful talent. In some spiritual houses she is known to transform into a buffalo or a gazelle, and she is also a master of disguise. One of the patakis about her describes this in detail.

Oya had come down into the world of the living. She arrived in the forest and, as she was known to do, assumed the form of a deer. There she wandered among the plants and animals for some time until she decided to take a trip to the market. Oya is also the owner of the marketplace and the commerce that occurs there. To prepare, she slipped off the deerskin to reveal the form of a striking woman. Gathering her many-colored cloths for sale, she traveled to market. There she was seen by the orisha Chango, king of fire. He immediately became enamored of her. He tried to get closer, but just as he approached, she retreated back to the forest. Not one to give up, Chango followed her and watched as she put the deerskin back on and ran away deep into the forest. Chango also loves a good chase, so now he was even more enchanted with her. A few days later, on market day, Chango returned to the forest to see if he could find Oya again. He saw her slide out of the deerskin, pick up her wares, and head out. Chango quickly grabbed the skin and hid it. Then he waited patiently for her to return. When she did, she was beside herself, frantic because she could not find her skin. Chango told Oya that he would return the skin if she promised to become his wife. Oya agreed, and from that point on they traveled together in the form of roaring thunder and flashing lightning. Chango has many wives and consorts, however, and their relationship is a colorful one.

One of my favorite stories about Oya and Chango tells how she tried to keep him at home by surrounding their house with skeleton sentries to scare him into staying. Despite his marriage to the queen of the cemetery, Chango is known to have a great fear of death. But his relationship with women is even more legendary. He fled from this difficult situation with the help of another one of his wives, Oshún. This orisha of love came to his aid, seduced the skeletons, and distracted them long enough for Chango to make his escape.

Chango does return to Oya again, however, for she is his favorite partner in battle. One of the most highly debated patakis concerns one occasion where they fought together against their enemies. Like with any good story there are always variations in the telling, but it goes a little something like this. Chango usually has his hand in many fights and battles. One day, he found himself at the mercy of his enemies, surrounded in the deep woods. He had run out of options. He was without his horse, without his soldiers, without even food or shelter. His persecutors continued, and things looked very bleak. Yet Chango continued to run through the forest without sleep or sustenance until he came to the home of Oya, one of his favorite wives.

Oya asked him what in the world was going on. Chango explained that his enemies had him surrounded, and he literally had nowhere else to turn. Despite his pride and machismo, he begged for her help. Oya told Chango to have courage, that she would find a solution. Her plan was for them to exchange not only clothes but even hair in order to deceive their enemies. It is said that Chango shaved his beard and gave it to Oya to wear. In return, she loaned him one of her dresses to wear as a disguise as he secretly crept past opposing lines. Those against them were bested on every level. Chango made it past them safely, and the sight of Oya wearing Chango's beard was a truly terrifying sight to behold. Even today one of Oya's praise names roughly translates to "she who grows a beard on account of war."

Hoodoo practices of the southern United States honor this energy in the form of Santa Marta. She is called upon for help in matters of love, and is specifically useful for reining in straying lovers, or kindling a new love. She's also been known to help with dominating your enemies. There are commercial preparations available as baths, candles, powders, and more for her. But as with all magick, be careful what you wish for, as everything comes with a price.

In Nigeria, Oya is connected to the Egungun masquerades. For some she is the only woman who can enter into these ancestor societies and practices. Just like the masqueraders, Oya is often wearing a mask. Some even believe that humans are unable to look on her true face.

I remember going for divination with my santo godmother to her godparents' house many year ago. Several of my godbrothers and godsisters and I awaited eagerly to find out our patron orisha. As usual, there was much speculation among us as to who would claim our heads. Now Oya doesn't seem to manifest as often as the other orishas these days, especially in a spiritual house dominated by children of Oshún, which ours was. So when we were waiting to find out who our godbrother would get, who was attractive, successful, and powerful, we all guessed he was an Oshún. But when he emerged from the room and told us that he had been told he was an Oya, it all seemed to make sense. He was a performer and costumer by profession, actually spending much of his time making masks. This is not an isolated phenomenon. Lately many people have developed a passion for orisha fashion. The late great fashion designer Alexander McQueen featured Eshu and several other Yoruba deities in his 2000 collection. Since then many others have followed suit, creating clothes, jewelry, and even tattoos for the orisha. Like many things in the religion, some condemn these practices, while others salute them.

There is another pataki of Oya that was recounted to me by a babalawo in the Ifa tradition, Robert Ogbe Di. In Odu Obara Kana, Orunmila, the orisha of divination, lived near a town inhabited by his enemies. Every day, he would read himself; and every day, he would mark ebo (rituals, offerings, and sacrifices determined through divination) in an attempt to resolve the situation. Despite making the ebos, his situation continued to worsen. His enemies would be knocked down for a bit, but soon enough they would be up to their old tricks again. Each orisha was called to help, and each orisha received ebo. Eleggua, Ogun, Shango, and Obatala each helped for a bit, but nothing seemed to solve the problem. Soon Orunmila's enemies would be after him again, causing problems and disturbing his life. In desperation, Orunmila cast Ifa and asked for a final solution to his problem. The advice was offered: "Call on Oya and ask her help."

Orunmila had not worked with Oya before, but in desperation he would try anything. When he called on Oya as instructed, a woman appeared whirling two black horsetails. She said, "All I want is a basket, two hens, and a few other things, and I will solve your problem."

This amazed Orunmila. He had offered goats and rams, adimú upon adimú (offering of food), but Oya laughed and said, "I don't need all that, because I am not like the other orisha. I walk my own way. Will you bring what I ask?"

Orunmila agreed. He had nothing to lose.

Oya smiled. "Go to bed. When you awaken, your problem will be solved."

Shaking his head, Orunmila went to bed.

When he awoke after a restful night's sleep, Orunmila went outside and stopped dead in his tracks. Where the town had been was only devastation. A tornado had come through in the night and cut a track through the town, destroying everything in its path. Everyone in the town had been swept away. The path of the tornado led right up to the edge of his property and stopped. As he stood there, dumbfounded, Oya appeared. "I have done as you asked. Where is my ebo?"

Orunmila was horrified. "But," he stammered. "This wasn't what I asked for at all! I just wanted you to get my enemies to leave me alone! I didn't want to kill them!"

Oya replied, "You are too soft-hearted for your own good. Some situations can only be resolved one way, and those are the ones I resolve. I told you, I walk my own way. Those enemies would have never stopped bothering you as long as they were alive; they would always come back, because they hated you. You found them annoying, but they found you detestable. Now, I have solved your problem. Where are my hens and basket?" Orunmila made ebo, and Oya went on her way, singing.

While each of these stories is told in a particular context, specifically as an explanation for divination, they do provide insight into the character of the orisha and how they function in the religions.

Oya in Creation

There are many representations of Oya, not just in art, but in music and dance as well. The popular musical duo Ibeyi has a successful song for this orisha called "Take Me Oya." In it they sing about catching the wind and the cloud. Oya is elusive and formidable, just like the wind itself. One of my favorite performers here in New York City is DJ Sabine Blaizin and OyaSound Productions, which according to her website highlights the "intersections of the cultures of the African diaspora through the syncretism of traditional rhythms and electronic music." If you have a chance to attend one of their events, I highly recommend it.

Images of Oya often feature her twirling her rainbow skirts of nine colors and wielding her horsetail whip. Many depict her with her face covered with a beaded veil and commanding her tools—lightning bolts. In 2017 I was blessed to be able to witness a performance piece honoring the orisha Oya by artist Clarivel Ruiz as part of the Art in Odd

Places festival in New York City. In the piece titled "Ase Oya," Oya herself manifested on the streets of New York to bless passersby with rose water and the Ashe of this orisha. There are also numerous sacred dances for Oya from Cuba that gracefully feature her horsetail whip, stirring up the power of the wind. The dancers spin and contort themselves at high speeds just like the whirlwind they are honoring.

Oya Herbs and Offerings

As the owner of both cemeteries and gardens, Oya enjoys many plants and botanicals. Just like the clothes she wears, her fruits and vegetables are often dark colored. Oya offerings are frequently laid out in red gourd bowls.

- Aniseed
- Camphor
- Carnations (purple or red)
- Cinnamon
- Dill
- Dittany of Crete (rare)
- Dragon's Blood
- Eggplants
- Flamboyant pods (royal poinciana)
- Geraniums
- Grapes (red or purple)
- Hibiscus
- Limes
- Marigolds
- Myrrh
- Oakmoss
- Papayas
- Plantains
- Plums (black)
- Pomegranates
- Raspberries
- Sandalwood
- Star apple
- Strawberries
- Yams

Oya Workings

There are many different workings that you may wish to undertake to better help your understanding and connection to this orisha of change. As always, keep in mind that you are undertaking these efforts to help bring about the best possible changes in the situation for you; the goal is to strengthen your relationship and honor the Ashe of Oya in all its power and glory.

OYA FLOOR WASH

To honor Oya, remove negativity, and bring about necessary change, wash down the floors, windowsills, and thresholds with this mixture. As Oya is the spirit of the wind, please leave your windows wide open as you are carrying out this wash. This will allow the energy to flow through your space.

Ingredients

- 1 cup rainwater
- 1 cup spring water
- 9 drops cypress oil
- 9 drops sandalwood oil
- 9 marigolds

Gather all ingredients on your working altar or shrine. Combine the waters and oils in a large bowl. Add the flowers one at a time. Stir counterclockwise nine times. Strain the mixture into a glass jar or bowl. Now it is ready to use.

Add 1 cup of the mixture to your regular wash water and use generously. When you are done, pour out the used wash water at the nearest crossroads. ■

OYA CANDLE

Use this candle for help in connecting to the ancestors and communicating with the dead. It is also useful when you need extra strength and courage.

Ingredients

- Dirt from the cemetery gates
- Oya image candle
- Pinch of dill
- 3 drops lime oil

Assemble all ingredients on your working altar or shrine. Place the dirt in the center of your space and put the candle on top of it. Put the dill on top of the candle and add the lime oil. Before lighting the candle, say one of the praise chants for Oya—"Hekua Oya" or "Hekua Hey Yansa"—nine times. The candle is now ready for use. ■

CEMETERY DIRT

To obtain cemetery dirt, knock three times and leave an offering at the cemetery gates. If you are able, take a small spoonful of dirt. Be sure to thank the spirits that reside there. The dirt can be used to connect to the ancestors and the spirit of the useful dead. ■

RED BEANS AND RICE

This is a traditional heritage dish cooked for both the ancestors and Oya. You may consider making it for her feast day, February 2.

Ingredients

- 4 cans red kidney beans, rinsed and drained
- 4 cups chicken stock
- 4 cups cold water
- 1 teaspoon apple cider vinegar
- 1 large onion, chopped
- 4 cloves garlic, minced
- 4 bay leaves
- 1 teaspoon dried thyme
- 1 teaspoon dried basil
- ¼ cup fresh parsley, chopped
- ½ teaspoon salt
- ½ teaspoon black pepper
- ½ teaspoon white pepper
- 2 or 3 hot peppers, chopped fine
- 1 pound cooked sausage, bacon, or ham, cubed
- 3 cups cooked white rice

Place beans in a saucepan with stock, water, vinegar, onion, garlic, spices, peppers, and pork. Bring to a simmer, stirring occasionally. Cook over low heat for 3 to 4 hours. Remove and discard bay leaves. Add more salt and pepper to taste. Serve over rice. Would be well paired with a Burgundy wine and French bread. Serves 10 to 12. ■

ROASTED YAMS WITH LIME

The yam, sweet potato's African cousin, has been celebrated for centuries in Ghana and Nigeria. They are the center of an entire festival focusing on ancestors, strength, and harvest. Because of this they make a wonderful offering for Oya.

Ingredients

- 4 large yams
- 2 tablespoons butter
- Juice of 2 limes

Preheat oven to 375 degrees. Rub yams with butter and wrap in foil. Bake for 45 to 60 minutes or until soft. Remove from oven, cut open, and top with a pat of butter and ½ teaspoon lime juice. Mash together, and season with salt and pepper to taste. Serves 4. ■

OYA PAPAYA SOUP

This recipe combines many of Oya's favorite food offerings. Again, it can be used as part of a larger ancestor offering or rite, or specifically for the orisha Oya to bring ingenuity to any situation.

Ingredients

- 1 teaspoon butter
- 1 green papaya, peeled, seeded, and cubed
- 1 medium red onion
- 1 cup chicken stock
- 1 cup vegetable stock
- Hot sauce to taste
- Salt and pepper to taste
- 1 cup heavy cream

Melt butter in a medium saucepan and add papaya and onion. Fry just until the mixture starts to brown. Add stock, hot sauce, and salt and pepper and cook over low heat until papaya is tender. Transfer to a food processor or blender and mix until the soup is smooth. Add ½ cup heavy cream. Mix until combined. Return soup to the saucepan and simmer for 5 minutes. Stir in remaining cream and remove from heat. Add additional salt, pepper, and hot sauce to taste. Serves 3 to 4. ■

Oya helps individuals put things into perspective. She wields the wind with a mighty whip, bringing destruction or gifts as she sees fit. Her wisdom and resourcefulness can turn around almost any situation. Her Ashe flows between this world and the next, helping us change what is necessary.

5

NANA BURUKU, THE WISDOM OF THE ANCIENTS

Fierce, strong, and an immensely powerful protector of women, Nana Buruku is a force for these times. In a way she almost transcends time itself, as one of the most ancient energies in the orisha pantheon. Nana Buruku, also called Nana Bouclou and Nana Buluku, is worshiped in Nigeria, Ghana, Togo, and Benin, and she even takes a sacred place in the pantheon of New Orleans Voodoo as well as Bahia, the seat of many Umbanda and Candomble practices. In some histories she is associated with the Nago spirits, and in others the Arara.

Theories abound about the origins of this powerful orisha. Some say she has no place in modern worship, while others insist she inserted herself into modern practices because she was needed. Her rites involve healing and herbalism. She is seen as a formidable reminder of tradition, dedication, love, and peaceful resolution.

In La Regla Lucumi she is seen as the mother, or sometimes grandmother, of the orisha Babaluaiye. One of the lesser known orishas, she is only rarely the subject of initiations and rituals. When she is, however, the instructions for honoring her are complex. Many of the specifications stem from her conflict with Ogun, which is described in one of the traditional patakis of the religion.

Nana Buruku was deep in the forest amid a thick grove of bamboo, watching all the animals and the birds enjoy their day, when she heard a giant noise. It was the orisha Ogun. He had entered the forest with his machete, intent on hunting the animals he found there. The ruckus he created scared the birds and caused many of the other animals to flee too. There was, however, a single deer left, and Ogun went after it with his blade. What he did not know was that Nana Buruku was there watching and in that moment transformed herself into a large snake. Just as he was about to kill the deer, Nana Buruku appeared in front of Ogun. Terrified, he quickly fled the scene and the deer was saved. The deer was immensely grateful and bestowed upon Nana Buruku the ability to use deer as a sacrifice to her. But in memory of the occasion, these sacrifices can only be made with a bamboo or wood knife. From that time forward, there has been a taboo against using any metal when dealing with Nana Buruku.

Some historians place this orisha as the mother of the divine twins Mawu and Lisa. This shows her connection to some of the practices that went on to flourish in Haiti and other parts of the Caribbean. Here these sacred twins are known as Marassa, and like Nana Buruku herself they seem to have existed since the start of time. Even some traditional folk songs tell of this relationship, describing how Nana Buruku created the twins, and then gave them the ability to handle human affairs while she went on to deal with bigger concerns.

In Hoodoo practice Nana Buruku is often equated with St. Anne. This is probably due to the fact that in the Bible Anne is the grandmother of Jesus Christ, and the mother of Mary. Nana Buruku's feast day is July 26. She is said to convey blessings of fertility and also protection for pregnant women. You can purchase candles, talismans, oils, and more that are dedicated to St. Anne and said to give protection to mothers, families, and small children. Other representations of Nana Buruku imagine her as a very old woman, the quintessential woman almost giving guidance for all things feminine and maternal. The color purple is most often associated with her. Thus, the elekes, or ritual necklaces, for her are usually lavender and white, or lavender and black. She is frequently shown with a veil partially over her face, usually made of straw or beads. These images also incorporate cowrie shells, which she takes as an offering. This shell from the watery depths is actually part of a tropical marine mollusk. It forms detailed spiral shapes, evoking its own natural magick in a simple yet complex way, just like the Ashe of Nana Buruku herself.

Herbs and Offerings for Nana Buruku

It can easily be said that all herbs and plants are owned by Nana Buruku. There are some, however, that are specifically used in formulas and as offerings to her:

- Cypress
- Garlic
- Juniper
- Marshmallow
- Mint
- Mullein
- Popcorn
- Sage
- Spanish moss
- Tobacco

Nana Buruku Workings

All workings involving Nana Buruku are serious. In her immense wisdom, she does not often trouble herself with matters of the living. There are, however, a few workings that can be done if needed.

NANA BURUKU POPCORN RITUAL BATH

The following bath is a traditional one used for healing and blessings from Nana Buruku. For most of us it may seem a bit unusual to fill a tub with popcorn, but this is how it is done. The best time for this working is on the full moon.

Ingredients

- ½ cup dried black-eyed peas
- Nana Buruku candle
- 3 tablespoons spring water
- 17 cups popcorn

Pour the black-eyed peas onto a ceramic or glass plate. Place the candle securely on top of them. Cover the beans with spring water. Then light the candle. Move the candle into a secure place in your bathroom.

Place the popcorn in your bathtub; then get in the tub. Focus on the negativity and illness leaving your body. Do this for as long as you feel comfortable.

When you are done, gather the popcorn in a bag and dispose of it on the earth or in moving water far from your home. After you leave it, turn around and do not look back.

Continue to burn the candle until it is done. As always, never leave a burning candle unattended. If you must, extinguish it and relight it as necessary until it is burnt down. ■

NANA BURUKU CANDLE

The past few years have seen numerous African-based images of this orisha. Many are available on candles. If you can't use one of these for your working, I suggest using a St. Anne candle or a plain 7-day purple candle in glass.

This working can help to connect with Nana Buruku and for struggles with motherhood and family.

Ingredients

- Candle to represent Nana Buruku
- 3 drops cypress oil
- Pinch of mullein
- Pinch of sage
- 3 juniper berries

Place the candle on your ritual altar or space. Light the candle in silence. After it has been burning for 10 to 15 minutes, add the oil, herbs, and berries. For best results, sit with the candle for some time in silence each day until it is done. Meditate on the issues you need to take to Nana Buruku. ■

SETTING A TABLE FOR NANA BURUKU

Remember, no metal is to be used on this altar or shrine, or in connection with the items placed there.

Ingredients

- Purple or white cloth (her color is most often purple)
- Image or statue used to represent Nana Buruku
- Candle for Nana Buruku or St. Anne

- Raven or crow feather (naturally molted)
- Living piece of bamboo in water
- Offering of food or fruit
- Drink offering

Gather all the necessary ingredients. Lay the cloth on the table. Set the image or statue in the center. Light the candle and place it in the space. If possible, play or sing the chant for Nana Buruku. There is a wonderful version by M. Portillo Dominguez and group put out by Smithsonian Folkways as part of the *Orishas Across the Ocean* collection, recorded in 1998. Next, place the feather and bamboo in a straw basket and present that along with the food and drink offerings. Your table is now active and ready for use. ■

Nana Buruku shows us with loving kindness what is truly important. She guides her children and family with a peaceful and powerful protective force. Many assert that Nana Buruku was one of the orishas that helped to guide individuals through the horrible slave trade. It is said she rode with them on the ships across the seas. Her children took turns protecting them: Lisa kept watch over the day, and Mawu looked out at night. These tales show us how Nana Buruku can help take us through the darkest times and tragedies and prepare for whatever lies ahead.

6

MAMI WATA, THE MOTHER OF WEALTH

Mami Wata is a mermaid, a mother, and a creator. She is one of the most ancient deities, and her worship dates back thousands of years. Images of her often have the body of a woman and the tail of a fish or reptile. In fact, she isn't just one deity, but instead represents thousands. Mami Wata is seen as all the water deities, all the divine waters coming together in harmony. Like the images that are chosen to represent her, she is simultaneously reptile and human, straddling the earth and water, bridging culture and nature; she is the sacred mistress of all waters.

Unlike the divinities we have looked at up to this point, Mami Wata is not an orisha. Because of her multifaceted nature, Mami Wata is frequently associated with the orisha Yemaya, the loa La Sirene, and the sirens of legend. However, people must be careful, as these are different and unique energies, and should always be viewed as such. Think of it as they may be composed of the same water sometimes, but they are not the same. Mami Wata is the sea water of Yemaya, but present in all other waters as well.

The domain of Mami Wata is primarily the healing waters, whose power can be applied to physical, emotional, spiritual, and even financial healing. Her devotees are blessed with great wealth in the form of money, opportunity, and knowledge. They are provided for bountifully in all aspects of their lives. Like many of the divinities in the African traditional religions, many of her elements have been overtly sexualized. The exoticized "other" has often been the focus of the Western male gaze, which has dominated traditional scholarship since its beginnings. However, her actual domain revolves around conception and motherhood.

I remember the first Mami Wata ceremony I ever took part in with the Voodoo Spiritual Temple and priestess Miriam, accompanied by the Dragon Ritual Drummers. I have been a member of the temple for over twenty-five years now, but this was in the early days, and I wasn't exactly sure what to expect. (I never really know what to expect in a ceremony, even today, but this was especially true in the beginning.) Preparations began long before the actual ceremony was scheduled to start. As someone new to the practice, the list of foods, offerings, and spiritual items required seemed endless. My godbrothers and I traveled back and forth the long and literally rocky road to the ritual site numerous times, trying to make sure everything was right for the rite. The ceremony was to take place on a beach on the edge of a large lake. I had yet to understand the true wisdom of this location. However, the candles nestled in the sand and shining bright under the light of the moon were truly sublime. Our songs, dances, drumbeats, and prayers would bridge these two sites—the water and the land. I have to admit that I was a bit apprehensive before things began. I had heard that Mami Water helped troubled mothers, and as a parent who lost a child, the gravity of the situation was not lost on me. What followed was one of the most powerful rites I have ever attended. We stood for hours, wading in the water and singing, dancing, and drumming to honor this powerful force.

Part of Mami Wata's formidable power comes from her connection to enslaved Africans and their numerous descendants throughout the world. It is as if the shared history and trauma strengthen the ancestral memory, even if the practices have been lost due to colonization and suppression.

Just as we see with some of the Haitian loa like Erzulie, some devotees in Nigeria are known to enter into a spiritual marriage with Mami Wata. These individuals are said to be "married in the water." Mami Wata very often manifests as gender-fluid and can be known to marry individuals of any gender. In addition to taking spouses, Mami Wata also has daughters. These are women who are said to have the appearance of Mami Wata. They are seen as very attractive, unique, and over the top. They frequently enter into conversations with spirits.

As I learned from experience, Mami Wata is the water that never takes a rest. Many say that those who have superior powers of divination are under the protection of Mami Wata. All forms of knowing the future—tarot reading, astrology, numerology, tea/coffee reading, clairvoyance, clairaudience, crystal divination, palm reading, and more—are her domain. It's as if she is connected to both the future and the past through her divine wisdom.

The Faces of Water

There may even within this name be many energies referred to as Mami Watas or Papi Watas. They have many faces and multiple manifestations. The fluidity of the energy of Mami Wata allows for it to exist with many varying elements. One unusual way that this has happened is its identification with some of the Hindu practices. In some cases, various Hindu images and offerings are used for her. I even remember one time where I was told to offer water from the river Ganges. It's almost as if water, being true to its nature, will seek its own level, on either the physical or spiritual plain.

Her equation with the serpent has led to Mami Wata often being represented by the Catholic image of Santa Marta in certain cultures. Santa Marta is frequently portrayed with a snake or a dragon. This association has sometimes led people to equate this energy with both negativity and sin, just like the serpent in the Garden of Eden. In other areas, such as Nigeria, there are often multiple images present on a shrine for

Mami Wata, which may include the crucified Christ and the Madonna and child. Some even equate Mami Wata with Christian beliefs and mores as a way of navigating the modern religious landscape and stigmas against more traditional and ancient religions.

In recent years the art world has taken a fancy with looking at the many manifestations of Mami Wata. There have been numerous books, articles, performances, and museum shows dedicated to her. At one such show, a patron even began to interact with the altar set up, leaving offerings of money, fruit, and coins.

The popular image of the double-tailed mermaid has also become associated with Mami Wata. There has been much controversy lately about this image being used both in a Pagan context and by a large coffee retailer. While the coffee retailer claims he found the design in an old Norse book, the origins of this depiction are still hotly debated among art historians. Some believe it was brought to West Africa by Portuguese sailors in the fifteenth century, but no matter what its origins, it was quickly adopted and transformed into its own thing among the Yoruba and neighboring kingdoms. These images frequently have long, flowing hair, which is representative of great wealth and power.

The image and character of Mami Water are also no stranger to the marketplace. In the early 1900s, Mami Wata's name and image found their way onto the bottles of the German perfume company Dralle. The label featured a mermaid gazing deeply into a magick mirror. Today she is associated with a water bottle company, although her image isn't used. Dare I say it, she's everywhere.

I recently had the opportunity to see Djimon Hounsou's long-awaited documentary about his homeland of Benin, *In Search of Voodoo: Roots to Heaven*. The cinematography in this film is phenomenal. It's almost as if the beauty of the religion can be felt through its sublime images. In the film, Hounsou highlights two beautiful ceremonies for Mami Wata in Grand Popo, a small town in southwest Benin renowned for its Voodoo practices. One ceremony takes place at the Mami Wata temple, the other at the water's edge. The viewer is allowed to see close up the priestesses of Mami Wata and how they sing, dance, and honor this divine feminine force. An interesting contrast is presented between the services at the temple and the more intimate one at the lagoon. At the lagoon people washed in the water, played in the sand, and danced with a free and vital energy, while the people at the temple were relegated to more regimented movements. The lagoon was almost a performance, while the other bursts forth as several participants even cross over into trance. Caution must be taken not to lose these possessed individuals to the water. The power of Mami Wata in all her sacred manifestations is always respected.

Recently Mami Wata has also begun to surface on the international pop music scene as well. Artists like N'Deye, Skip & Die, as well as Sa-Roc all have popular songs dedicated to her. Each one shows a different way of honoring Mami Wata in song be it traditional chant, or even a rap lyric. This inclusion of an ancient goddess in a modern context truly shows her lasting power and influence in every possible sphere.

Offerings for Mami Wata

- Coffee
- Kola nut
- Milk
- Palms
- Rice
- Yams

In addition to the above foods, Mami Wata is also offered small boats, mirrors, and alcohol. Many of the offerings are specific to the regions where she is honored, including local fruits and vegetables.

The manifestations of Mami Wata are deep and powerful, like the oceans and rivers she resides in. The following recipes and formulas will help you to get in touch with the resolve, strength, and majesty that reside within Mami Wata.

MAMI WATA RITUAL BATH

Take this bath whenever you want to connect with the great power of Mami Wata. It will help you to still your mind, and also give you guidance and direction in your life. Create the mixture on the eve of the new moon and then you can take the bath whenever necessary. Make sure your tub and bathroom are clean. This will allow the purest and best blessings to find their way directly to you.

Ingredients

- 1 cup sea water
- 1 cup river water
- 3 cowrie shells
- 1 teaspoon seaweed
- 1 teaspoon sea salt
- 3 drops lemon oil
- 3 drops gardenia oil

Place all the items in a large glass jar on your altar, and shake well. Carefully toss the glass into the air and catch it, to charge it with the energy of the spirit world. Then leave it overnight where the light of the moon will touch it. The mixture is then ready to use. Place a small amount into your bath whenever needed. Use the mixture within 2 weeks; then make more if necessary. ■

MAMI WATA DIVINATION CANDLE

Those who perform divination have an extra special connection to Mami Wata. Divination skills are vital for all spiritual people—guidance from the divine is important in all that you do—but like all skills, they must be strengthened. Use the following candle on the full moon to help increase your success and knowledge.

Ingredients

- Blue 7-day candle
- 3 drops copal oil
- 3 drops myrrh oil
- 3 drops sandalwood oil
- 7 cowrie shells

Gather all the ingredients on your working altar or ritual space. Using a toothpick, poke three holes in the top of the candle. Add the oils to the candle and swirl in a clockwise direction to make sure the oil is filling each of the holes. Then light the candle and surround the base with the cowrie shells in a circle on the altar or shrine. Play a chant for Mami Wata, or simply ocean sounds, as you still your mind and focus on the flame before you. Put the candle out every evening and then light it again the next day, making sure you are safe and not leaving the burning candle unattended. Continue this each night until the candle has burned down. Pay special attention to your dreams at this time, as they may be likely to bring prophecies revealed. ■

SOKOURA OR FUFU FOR MAMI WATA

Ceremonies for Mami Wata are frequently associated with feasting. Fufu is a traditional African recipe made with yams, one of her staple foods. West African yams are frequently longer and have white flesh, so if you don't have an African market available to you, do your best to find the right type of tuber. Many people these days use cassava or yam flour to make fufu, but with a blender or food processor it is possible to make your own from actual yams.

Ingredients

- 3 pounds yams, peeled and cubed
- Water
- ½ teaspoon salt
- ½ teaspoon pepper
- 2 teaspoons olive oil or butter

Fill a large saucepan with water and bring to a boil. Add yams and cook until tender, about 40 minutes. Drain. Add salt, pepper, and olive oil or butter, and mash with a hand masher. Transfer yams to a food processor or blender and blend until there are no lumps, but stop before the mixture becomes a puree. This is meant to be served with a spicy sauce or as an accompaniment to a stew or soup. ■

SETTING A TABLE FOR MAMI WATA

You may wish to set up a table, or shrine, for Mami Wata. This will help you get in touch with the powerful feminine energy she embodies. Her color is very often blue, and you can see that reflected in the offerings here.

Items

- Blue cloth
- Florida Water
- Statue or image of Mami Wata
- Blue candle holder
- Blue votive candle
- Bottle of ocean water
- Bottle of river water
- Bottle of spring water
- Bottle of lake water
- Seashells
- Starfish
- Other offerings from the water

Prepare your ritual space by making sure it is clean and clear. Cover the area with a blue cloth and sprinkle it with Florida Water. Then position the statue or image in the center of your shrine. In front of this, place the candle holder. Put a small amount of water in the bottom of the candle holder; then put the candle on top. Light the candle. Next, arrange the waters and other items around the candle and statue or image. The space is now ready for use. ■

Mami Wata represents the waters of life in every form. The oceans, the seas, the rivers, the lakes, and even our own bodies contain sacred water. By welcoming this goddess into your life, you can connect to this ancient power. She can provide gifts of prophecy, material wealth, joy, and bounty.

7

ERZULIE, THE SWEET WATERFALL OF PASSION AND THE STORM OF LOVE

Like many of the powerful feminine forces we have been looking at, the Haitian loa Erzulie has several different avatars. Also called Ezili, this spirit of love can come forward as Erzulie Danto, Erzulie Freda Dahomey, Erzulie Ge Rouge, Erzulie Mansur, Erzulie Toho, Erzulie Dayila, Erzulie Mapyang, Erzulie Taureau, and oh so many more. Like many of the loas and orishas in this book, Erzulie is also thought to have many marriages or relationships, including one with the serpent creator Damballa Wedo and another with the warrior Ogou. She is frequently paired with these in both the art and prayers of the tradition. We see the Erzulies manifest in New Orleans Voodoo and Haitian Vodou practices.

In New Orleans Voodoo we have a loa known as Erzulie Freda Dahomey. She is also ever present in Haitian Vodou, and as her name implies was historically honored among the Dahomey people in west Africa. Her color is pink, and she is said to cry the tears of the world because people simply don't do the right thing. She wants people to be better: to be honest, truthful, respectful, considerate, and kind. Some people say that this Erzulie was one of the ruling loa, or guardians, of Voodoo Queen Marie Laveau, whom we'll discuss later on. This Erzulie claims the magick mirror as one of her ritual tools. This loa can see into the visible and invisible worlds, and blur the line between them when necessary.

Erzulie Danto, alternatively known as Ezili Dantor, is also a part of both the Haitian Vodou and New Orleans Voodoo pantheon. She belongs to the Petro Nanchon, or Nation. Vodou hounfor (temples) honor her with the colors red, blue, and gold. Her colors mimic that of the Haitian flag and also those used for Santa Barbara Africana. Most often she is pictured as a dark-skinned woman, and images of St. Barbara Africana are used to represent her on altars and shrines. Erzulie Danto is viewed as a powerful protector and defender of women. Some say she is a patron of LGBTQ individuals, and/or abused women and children. A stern mother, she is also a strict disciplinarian. While her offerings and sacrifices are not always as grand as the other loas, she does demand absolute devotion and dedication. She is traditionally honored on Tuesday, the day for honoring the Petro loa, or on Saturday. If her qualifications are met, she is known to bless her children with great abundance and success.

In Haitian Vodou, the Erzulies frequently enter into spirit marriages. These marriages, called Maryaj loa, are agreements between an individual and the loa where blessings are exchanged. People in some instances go through an actual wedding ceremony, exchanging rings and even signing a marriage license. Individuals then promise to devote themselves to that loa on a particular day of the week. There are even stories of people dedicating a room in their home to that loa and sleeping in it on that specific night. In return, the loa can be known to grant love, blessings, and guidance on every level. These arrangements can be temporary or permanent affairs. While all promises in the religion are important, those who have entered into a spirit marriage with Erzulie Danto must be extra careful, for when she is angered she is said to cause trouble with the authorities on every level, including police, government, and even the IRS. This is another reason that I advise people to find a spiritual house to join. They will be able to provide insight and guidance when dealing with all the delicate aspects of the loa.

Despite the fact that they are both Erzulies, many devotees believe that there is an intense rivalry between Erzulie Danto and Erzulie Freda Dahomey. They are seen as sisters who are always at odds. Most often people say they fought over a man, namely Ogou.

Arts of Erzulie

Haitian art and artists are world renowned for their depictions of loa in all their glory. In Haitian Vodou, art is intricately connected to the spiritual practices. Even before the rituals and ceremonies begin in this religion, the space is prepared with drawing called a veve. No one is precisely sure how they initially came to be, but popular folklore abounds on the topic. Some believe that veves were created originally from patterns formed in the dirt by chickens and other animals during ceremony. I have spoken to some scholars who believe that they are cross-cultural symbols from the cosmos. Whatever their origins, they are an integral part of the Vodou tradition.

A veve is most often drawn on open earth with cornmeal, flour, or coffee. In some spiritual houses, the person drawing the veve is supposed to use both hands, to symbolize the pathways into the world of the visible and the invisible. In other houses, individuals hold the materials in one hand and do the drawing with the other. I have also heard of some houses that throw the bowl of flour or cornmeal gently into the air before they begin creating, while others simply blow a pinch of the drawing material into the air when they are done. Clearly the practices can take many different forms, unique to each specific instance and locale.

Haitian Vodou rituals are most commonly situated around the *poteau mitan* (center pole), which forms another road for the divine to travel upon. Customarily, veves are drawn around the base of these poles. The elaborate creations are both beautiful and powerful to behold. A large part of the magick and mystery of the power of Haitian Vodou is accessed through repetition. This can take the form of veves. The veves are blessed and activated by sprinkling with rum, Florida Water, and other items. One thing that makes these ritual ground drawings unique is that they are meant to be walked on, danced on barefoot, and interacted with. It's almost as if they become a living part of the ceremony. I remember one occasion where the veve appeared to come alive, and actually seemed to be pulling us toward the ground.

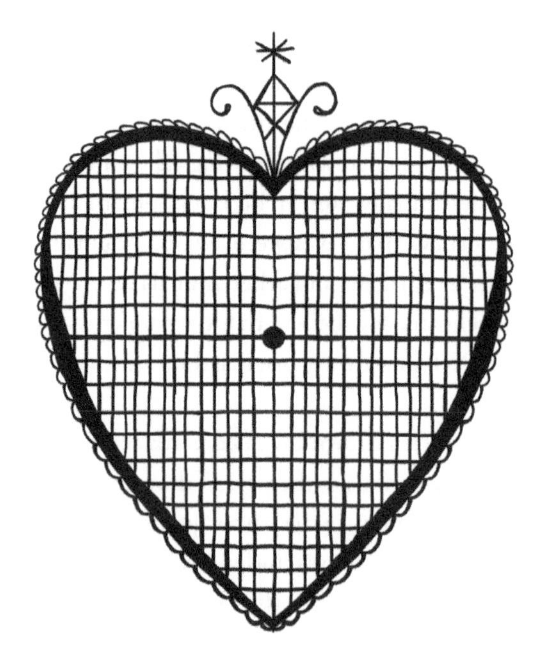

The veves for the Erzulies have fascinated insiders and outsiders to the religion since the very beginning. The most comprehensive book examining these ritual art forms, Milo Rigaud's *Ve-Ve*, depicts many different veves for the Erzulies. One of the most beautiful things about veves, however, is that they are ever evolving. They can transform because of the situation, or even be layered and expanded upon when needs must.

Most of the veves featuring Erzulie contain a heart. In the case of Erzulie Freda, the ritual drawings often feature latticework across the heart, as in the veve above. This possibly symbolizes the boundless nature of Erzulie's love and blessings. Some of the veves for Erzulie Danto feature latticework as well, but most often they have daggers or knives as part of the design.

Veves are, thankfully, not limited only to their cornmeal form. Metal veves are also popular in Haiti. In the 1800s, the veves began to be transformed to a new medium—recycled metal. A temporary ground drawing became a more permanent piece of art. In the ultimate upcycle, artists took metal from the Iron Market in Port-au-Prince, Haiti, and transformed it into offerings for the gods. One of the earliest artists working in this medium was the Haitian Georges Liautaud, born in Croix-des-Bouquets, in 1899. He dedicated himself to producing fascinating sculptures in the 1950s, and many generations of artists have continued to honor the loas with these fabulous creations. Recently, I was gifted a wall veve for Erzulie from a modern artists' collective in Port-au-Prince. If you do obtain one of these pieces, please do your best to make sure that artist was fairly compensated.

Another way in which veves have been transformed is in the creation of drapo Vodou, or Haitian Vodou flags. Drapo Vodou are probably one of the most recognized components of the religion. They have become a folk-art treasure throughout the globe. Just as with other forms of the veve, these are seen as living components of the religion, representations of the divine made manifest. They are saluted, held, danced with, and sung to.

Most temples have a least two flags to use for rites and ceremonies, honoring one if not two Erzulies. Flags for Erzulie Danto most often feature her colors of blue, red, gold, or black. They include a veve or image for the loa. The veves frequently feature her ritual dagger, knife, or sword, and Catholic images like St. Barbara Africana or the Black Madonna can also be used. The Black Madonna, known as Our Lady of Czestochowa, was said to have been brought to Haiti by Polish soldiers who fought for Napoleon in the early 1800s and quickly found themselves on the side of the black and indigenous people there. In some of these Catholic images a child is featured. This child is known as Anaise, or Anais.

Anaise, the Black Madonna's daughter, is said to function as a divine translator for Erzulie Danto. Flags for Erzulie Freda show this regal "Mademoiselle" in all her glory. She often is featured wearing a tiara and gold rings on her fingers, like a princess. The Catholic image of Mater Dolorosa is most often used to represent her. The flags are often colored baby pink or light blue. Her romantic focus is played out with her jewelry and clothing in this medium.

The Erzulies are also featured prominently on another variety of Haitian Vodou art: the *boutey*, or spirit bottle. A boutey is an upcycled glass bottle ornately decorated with sequins, feathers, and images of a loa. Traditionally these are left on the altar or shrine for the loa and used in offerings and ceremonies. Most often these bottles are in keeping with the ritual colors for the loa. The boutey for Erzulie Dantor are most often a deep blue, accented with red and gold. They can have sequins, tassels, and other decorations. Veves and Catholic lithographs are also incorporated in the designs. The same is true for Erzulie Freda Dahomey. However, her colors are baby pinks and gold, and elegant perfume bottles might be used. Most of the bottles I have come across feature Erzulie Freda Dahomey's lattice veve and are truly beautiful.

Erzulie is found over and over again in art, music, dance, and literature. Many see her as a loa of resistance and empowerment for all women. Dance legend and pioneer Katherine Dunham studied the dances of Haitian Vodou extensively and described Erzulie's dances as an "attitude." This attitude comes through both in the dances of Erzulie Danto, which are almost violent, and the ones for Erzulie Freda Dahomey which are coquettish and more delicate.

The ritual songs and prayers for Erzulie Danto also illustrate her resolve and fierceness. One tells of how she sustained seven stabs and still kept on fighting. She is also said to carry a ritual dagger. Popular stories tell us that she was attacked by a dagger during the Haitian revolution, and it was used to sever her tongue. Because of this, her language is often strained. In possession trance she is sometimes known to appear and vomit blood. There is nothing about this loa that is not intense.

Unlike many of the other loas, the drum rhythms for Erzulie, according to anthropologist Zora Neale Hurston, are not played during her rites. There is no shortage, however, of ritual music for her. Erzulie's songs tell her sacred story. In some of them, devotees call out, "Erzulie, where are you?" as they search deeply for this watery loa. Many call out to her, lamenting their troubles and asking for assistance. One of the most famous songs for Erzulie was written by Auguste de Pradines, also known as Kandjo, in the 1890s. It is still played as part of her sacred repertoire today. Many modern musicians have also added songs for Erzulie to their canon. Canadian singer Alannah Myles has the popular "Mistress of Erzulie," where she talks about a New Orleans Voodoo encounter. Then there is the jazz master Cecil Taylor, from New York City, who titled his 1989 album *Erzulie Maketh Saint*. One of my modern favorites is "Erzulie" by Monvelyno and Riva Precil. They are an amazingly powerful pair, and if you have the chance to listen to them in person, I highly recommend it. You may wish to play any or all of these tunes as you turn to Erzulie for inspiration and guidance.

Herbs and Offerings for Erzulie Freda Dahomey

- Baby's breath
- Bananas
- Basil
- Cardamom
- Cinnamon
- Gold jewelry
- Lace
- Makeup
- Perfume
- Pineapple
- Pink roses
- Sweet plantains
- White grapes

SETTING A TABLE FOR ERZULIE FREDA DAHOMEY

When working with Erzulie Freda, be sure everything is clean. This means your space, your ritual tools, and especially yourself. This Erzulie will not tolerate anything unclean in her presence. Make sure your dishes are done, and your entire body is clean, and even better perfumed, before setting out her offerings or trying to do any work with her.

Components

- Florida Water
- Pink lace cloth
- Flour or cornmeal to create a veve
- Statue or image of Erzulie Freda Dahomey
- Pink roses
- Baby's breath
- Pink candle

Cleanse your space thoroughly with Florida Water. Play music or sing a chant for Erzulie Freda Dahomey. Cover the area with the pink lace cloth, and feel free to add additional satin, silk, or lace pink cloth to make sure the base is beautiful. If you like, you may create a veve for Erzulie Freda Dahomey in flour or cornmeal on the ground under or in front of your space. Once your space is set, you may wish to dance on the veve in order to activate it and strengthen your connection to Erzulie Freda Dahomey. Next, place the statue or image of the loa in the center of the space. Arrange the flowers next to this. Finally, carve a veve for Erzulie Freda Dahomey into the candle, and light it. ■

ERZULIE FREDA DAHOMEY OIL

The following formula is designed to honor Erzulie Freda and to draw the best possible romance and pleasure to you.

Ingredients

- 1 ounce sweet almond oil
- 7 drops rose oil
- 7 drops ylang-ylang oil
- 3 drops cinnamon oil
- 3 drops sweet pea oil

Add all ingredients to a small bottle; then rub the oil bottle quickly between your hands to charge it with your energy. Leave it on your Erzulie Freda table or shrine overnight to bless it with her Ashe. If you don't have a dedicated space for this loa, you can leave the oil bottle outside overnight, or on a windowsill during the full moon. After you have done this, the oil is ready for use. ■

CINNAMON SPICE RICE FOR ERZULIE FREDA DAHOMEY

This delicious rice for Erzulie Freda Dahomey makes a perfect offering, as well as a great addition to your feast table. If you want a shortcut, add a bag of spiced chai tea to the cooking water with the rice instead of using the cinnamon and basil.

Ingredients

- 1 ½ cups water
- 1 teaspoon cinnamon
- 1 teaspoon dried basil
- 2 tablespoons butter
- 1 cup jasmine rice

Heat water in a medium saucepan. When the water starts to boil, add the cinnamon, basil, butter, and rice and stir. Reduce heat to simmer. Cover the pan and cook for 18 to 20 minutes or until almost all the water is evaporated. Remove from heat and let stand for 5 minutes; then fluff rice with a fork. Serves 4. ■

Herbs and Offerings for Erzulie Dantor

Offerings for Erzulie Danto are numerous and varying. They may include any of the following:

- Clairin (native rum distilled in Haiti)
- Creme de cacao
- Daggers
- Dolls
- Florida Water
- Griot (fried pork)
- Perfume
- Red grapes
- Red wine
- Rice and peas
- Silver chains and necklaces
- Sweet potatoes
- Tangerines
- Unfiltered cigarettes
- Yams

SETTING A TABLE FOR ERZULIE DANTOR

You may wish to create this type of table or shrine for the feast day for Erzulie Dantor, or whenever you feel a particularly strong connection to her.

Components

- Florida Water
- Red and/or blue cloth
- Veve, image, or statue for Erzulie Dantor
- Red or blue candle
- Unfiltered cigarettes
- Small dagger or knife
- Food offering
- Clairin or other Haitian rum

Gather all ingredients on your desired space. Clean the space by wiping it down or sprinkling it with Florida Water. Sing a chant or play music for Erzulie Dantor as you are creating the ritual table. Cover the space with the cloth. Place the veve, image, or statue of Erzulie Dantor in the center of the space. If you like, you may wish to also create the veve in flour or cornmeal on the ground under or in front of your space. Place the candle, cigarettes, dagger, and food offering on the cloth. If possible, take the rum into your mouth and spray the entire area with the rum. If you are unable to do this, simply pour some rum into a glass and leave it on the cloth. Light the candle. ■

ERZULIE DANTOR CANDLE

Some scholars believe that Erzulie Dantor's name comes from the phrase "D'en Tort," which illustrates this particular Erzulie's power as a righter of wrongs. This candle is created to help right the wrongs in your life.

Ingredients

- Veve for Erzulie Dantor
- Red or blue candle
- Candle holder
- Image or statuary for Erzulie Dantor
- Red rose petals
- Small dagger
- Shot of rum

Assemble all items on your working altar or sacred space for Erzulie Dantor. Carefully carve the veve for Erzulie Dantor into the front of the candle. Place the candle into the holder and set it in the center of your working space. If you are using an image, place it under the candle; if you are using a statue, place it behind the candle. Surround the items with red rose petals and place the dagger in the front of the statue. Take the shot of rum into your mouth and spray the entire area. If you are unable to do this, simply sprinkle the rum around your sacred space. Light the candle and speak aloud the wrongs you wish to be set right. ■

GRIOT FOR ERZULIE DANTOR

These tasty bites are a traditional Haitian treat and a classic offering for this loa.

Ingredients

- 1 pound baked ham, cubed
- 1 red onion, diced
- 3 scallions, sliced
- ½ teaspoon dried thyme
- ½ cup freshly squeezed orange juice
- ½ cup freshly squeezed lime juice
- 1 hot pepper, deveined, seeded, and chopped fine
- 2 garlic cloves, minced
- 1 cup flour
- ½ teaspoon cinnamon
- ½ teaspoon onion powder
- ¼ teaspoon cumin
- ¼ cup grapeseed oil

Place the cubed ham in a large ceramic or glass bowl; add ham, onion, scallions, thyme, orange and lime juice, hot pepper, and garlic and mix well. Cover with plastic wrap and chill overnight or at least 8 hours.

Remove the mixture from the refrigerator and warm in a nonreactive saucepan. Heat, stirring occasionally, for 30 to 45 minutes, or until most of the liquid has cooked down.

Remove ham with a slotted spoon and set aside to cool completely.

In a separate bowl, combine flour, cinnamon, onion powder, and cumin. Mix well. Coat the ham in the flour mix. In a frying pan, heat the oil over medium heat. Fry the breaded cubes on all sides until browned. Drain on paper towels. Serve with hot sauce or other Haitian dipping sauce. ■

The Erzulies are powerful manifestations of the sacred feminine who have important lessons about love to share with us. They urge us to explore both reality or retribution when the time is right.

8

AIDA WEDO, THE SHINING CROWN OF THE RAINBOW

Even those who know very little about Haitian Vodou seem to be familiar with the tale of the serpent and the rainbow. Sacred stories traverse boundaries and limitations, and this story of two divine snakes is no exception. For many devotees, the loas Damballa Wedo and Aida Wedo are the father and mother of Haitian Vodou and New Orleans Voodoo. They are part of the Rada family of loas, which tells of their origin in Dahomey, a kingdom in western Africa, now part of Benin. Both Aida Wedo and her husband Damballa Wedo are known to be immensely powerful. Despite the fact that many Haitian Vodou followers believe in a monotheistic god, commonly referred to as Bondye, in many ways Damballa and Aida Wedo are seen as creators—not just of Vodou, but of humankind.

Their legendary story is as follows: In a time before time, there were two sacred serpents—a male and a female. They were lovers, intertwined souls, who danced their magick on the continent of Africa. There came a time when that was no longer possible. War and strife made that possibility, and the push toward a new land a real necessity. The serpents made the long journey to the New World, namely North America and the Caribbean. Damballa Wedo made the trip beneath the seas, the realm of the ancestors and deep wisdom, while Aida Wedo traveled across the sky along the crown of the rainbow. They met, and in a strong embrace intertwined again in the New World, bringing the joy and beauty of their divine majesty.

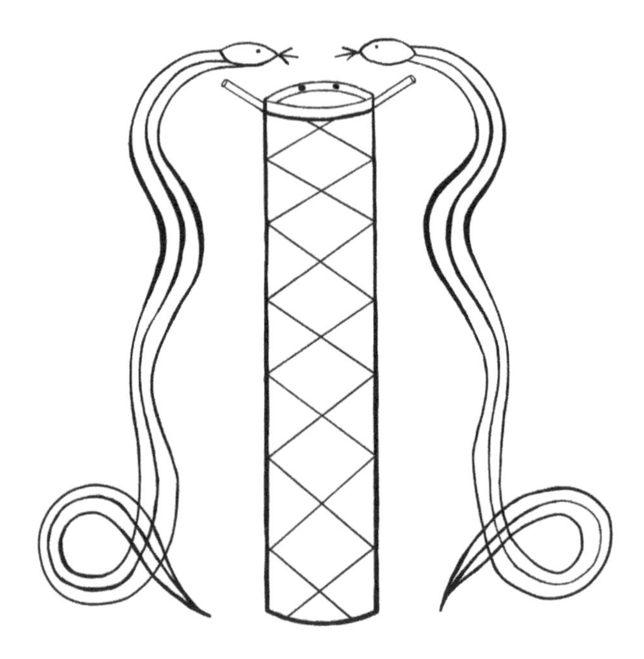

Aida Wedo represents the rainbow after the storm. She gloriously embodies the beauty of possibility. Many years ago, I performed a large public ceremony at a Pagan event for Aida Wedo. I asked people when we began to try to imagine things better than they could possibly imagine. As part of the rite, I asked them to see themselves in lives greatly improved, with all the successes they had ever dreamed of. I wasn't expecting it, but many people had a very hard time doing this. It seemed to be easier for them to envision a life full of despair than one of great joy and infinite possibility. In many ways this made me sad, and it also made me realize why so many of us struggle to have the better things in life. What happened to possibility? What happened to hope? Where have all the rainbows gone? Now this story serves as a cautionary tale to remind people that a positive outlook will always improve your chances of success, and that sometimes you need to stop limiting yourself and get out of your own way.

Snakes have been connected to magick since the very beginning. Some cultures believe that each time a snake sheds its skin, a completely new snake is born. It's as if they are ever transforming. Even though the process is less dramatic, humans are ever changing too. Aida Wedo can sometimes manifest in possession trance as this snake, with devotees writhing on the ground. Despite what is presented by mainstream media, possession is actually a sacred interchange between the individual, called a horse, and the loas, who come down and ride with important information and blessings for the individual.

Aida Wedo urges us to embrace all the changes in our lives. In Haitian Vodou she is almost always accompanied by her powerful husband Damballa Wedo. They travel together, reminding us of the importance of balance in all things. Many are familiar with the concept of yin and yang; this is an African-based cosmic balance where these snakes mimic and complement each other throughout time and space.

Aida Wedo in Creation and of Creation

Aida Wedo is often seen as a loa of creation. She is a divine mother who is responsible for birthing all of humanity. As such, she is frequently honored in Haitian art and music. Because of her role as creatrix, she is often featured on drapo Vodou, or sacred flags. Many of these mimic the veves for her, which frequently have two serpents rising up the poteau mitan (center pole), or a cross. A boutey for Aida Wedo is often decorated with snakes and rainbows made of sequins or fabric.

One of the most popular traditional Haitian dances performed for Aida Wedo, Damballa Wedo, and the Erzulies is called the Yanvalou. It is a dance of resistance, rebellion, and reclaiming. Its full-body movements echo those of a snake, with every muscle dedicated to undulating, rolling, and sliding into a new space. It is an ecstatic dance desired to transcend time and place. Some translate the name to mean "supplication," but whatever you call it, it is designed to give honor and respect to the loa with every muscle of the body.

Offerings for Aida Wedo

This loa is honored with all things white, representing peace, purity, and pure clarity. When possible, these white items are painted, or otherwise decorated in rainbow colors.

- Cotton
- Cream
- Flour
- Milk
- Rice
- Snake vertebrae
- Tamarind
- White eggs painted rainbow colors
- White flowers
- White snake sheds
- Wormwood

SETTING A TABLE FOR AIDA WEDO

Aida Wedo is honored in Haitian Vodou either on Mondays or Tuesdays. Creating this sacred space will help you to honor Aida Wedo, and hopefully welcome a rainbow of possibility into your own life. I find it particularly helpful for those individuals who are struggling with optimism and accepting necessary change.

Components

- Spring water
- Florida Water
- White cloth
- Rainbow cloth
- White flour
- White egg painted rainbow colors
- White 7-day candle
- Rainbow 7-day candle
- White flowers

Clean your sacred space with spring water and Florida Water. Sing a song for Aida Wedo or play the rhythm of the Yanvalou. Place a white cloth down on the space, and then lay the rainbow cloth over it. Place a white bowl in the center of the space and fill it with a small amount of white flour. Place the painted egg on the flour in the center of the bowl. Place the white candle on the left side of the table and the rainbow candle on the right side. Remove the white flowers from their stems and place them on the table as well. Do your best to quiet your mind. This means turning off the phone, television, and other electronics. Light the candles and meditate on your best dreams becoming reality. ■

AIDA WEDO SNAKE OIL

Snake oil has a reputation for being something sold by hucksters and charlatans, but this formula couldn't be further from that connotation. In fact, this Aida Wedo snake oil recipe helps you to find truth and justice in situations where you may be facing problems. It can help lead you to the rainbow after your personal storms, and see that sacred possibilities lie just around the bend.

Ingredients

- 3 drops cinnamon oil
- 3 drops galangal oil
- 3 drops gardenia oil
- 3 drops lime oil
- 13 drops sweet almond oil
- Small piece white snakeskin

Combine all ingredients into a glass bottle. Cover tightly. Rub quickly between your hands to charge the mixture with your energy. Then take a long, slow, deep breath and exhale it onto the bottle. It is now ready for use. Wear when you are facing difficulty and need a positive outlook. ■

DEVILED EGGS FOR DAMBALLA AND AIDA WEDO

Eggs are one of the most common offerings for Damballa and Aida Wedo. Used in many African traditional religions, eggs are said to represent both healing and new beginnings. The following recipe could be made as part of a mangé loa, a ceremonial feast common in Haitian Vodou that literally means "feeding the gods." Traditionally, these contained sacrifices, along with cooked foods, veves, songs, and dances for the loa.

Ingredients

- 9 hard-boiled eggs, chilled
- ¼ cup mayonnaise
- 1 tablespoon minced chives
- 1 tablespoon minced parsley
- 1 tablespoon minced dill
- 1 tablespoon minced basil
- 1 tablespoon relish
- ½ teaspoon dry mustard

- ½ teaspoon smoked paprika
- ¼ teaspoon onion powder
- ¼ teaspoon garlic powder
- Salt and pepper to taste

Boil eggs in water for approximately 20 minutes. Remove from heat, cover with cold water, and remove from shells. Slice each egg in half and scoop out the yolks. Place yolks in a large bowl and mash with a fork. Add mayonnaise and mix well. Then add chives, parsley, dill, basil, relish, mustard, paprika, onion powder, and garlic powder. Stir well to combine; then add salt and pepper to taste. Using a pastry bag or a spoon, fill the eggwhite shells with the yolk mixture. Top with additional parsley and paprika if desired. Serves 9. ■

ORGEAT SYRUP

This traditional syrup has been used as an offering at feasts and ceremonies for over a hundred years. Its ingredients and color make it perfect for pouring over cake or adding to drinks for Damballa and Aida Wedo.

Ingredients

- 2 cups blanched almonds, chopped
- 1 ½ cups water
- 1 ½ cups sugar
- 1 teaspoon orange flower water
- 1 teaspoon rose water
- 1 ounce rum

Place almonds into a food processor and pulse until ground. Warm sugar in a saucepan over medium heat and gradually add the water, stirring until combined. When it starts to boil, turn the heat down to low and add the almonds. Cook for 2 to 3 minutes, stirring constantly. Just before the mixture begins to boil again, cover and remove from heat. Let cool overnight.

Strain the mixture twice through a double piece of cheesecloth. Discard chopped almonds, or save for another use. Then add the orange flower water, rose water, and rum. Pour into a bottle and refrigerate. Keeps for up to 2 weeks. ■

AIDA WEDO GRIS-GRIS BAG

Gris-gris bags, also known as medicine bags, charm bags, or sorcerer's hands, have been used for centuries to make a portable magick to take with you wherever you go. You may wish to carry this gris-gris bag to honor Aida Wedo, and to help you have the confidence to manifest rainbows after your personal storms. Some female devotees choose to carry the bag in their bra so it will be close to their heart chakra, while others put it in the left pocket of their clothes, or around their neck.

Ingredients

- Small white candle
- 3 cotton balls
- Sprig of baby's breath
- White rose petals
- 1 teaspoon white flour
- 1 teaspoon tamarind powder

Gather all the items or your working altar or ritual space for Aida Wedo. Light the white candle. Add the cotton, baby's breath, rose petals, flour, and tamarind to a small bowl. Mix well with your hands. Place the mixture into a white natural cloth bag. Leave the bag in front of the candle until it is extinguished. Once the candle has finished burning, the bag is ready for use. ■

Aida Wedo is an ancient loa, powerful and kind. She may assist you when things appear to be at their most difficult. She moves ever so slowly and precisely. Aida Wedo shows us that possibility and change can be right around the bend, and things can be better than we have ever imagined.

9

LA SIRENE, THE SONG OF DESTINY, AND AYIZAN, THE PRIESTESS OF PLACE

Both La Sirene and Ayizan are very important loa in the pantheons of Haitian Vodou and New Orleans Voodoo. In many ways they are indicative of the highs and lows of this world. They are powerful feminine forces that help us realize how to navigate the difficulties of life.

La Sirene

One of the widely celebrated loa of Haitian Vodou is La Sirene, also called Lasirèn, Lasireen, and La Sirenn. She is part of the Rada family of loas, and her domain is the sea. Like the sirens of legend, she rules over all sacred sounds. This loa is called and given tribute with the sacred sound of the conch shell. La Sirene is almost always accompanied by Agwe. Some say she is his wife, others his devoted daughter. She is also frequently accompanied by her counterpart La Balenn, represented by the whale. When pleased, she can reward her devotees with great wealth and strong protection. Foremost, legend and lore tell us of her great beauty and vanity.

Many tell stories of La Sirene and how she takes people and sweeps them under the water. In some cases they don't return for several hours, or even days. This is seen by some as La Sirene claiming her children. Her song and beauty lure people to the depths of the water. After these watery transformations, individuals then possess both the mysteries and blessings of La Sirene, and sometimes they sleep with the mermaids. In many cases the appearance of these people is changed too; their hair is straighter, and their skin lighter.

Many have written about the skin color of La Sirene, as she frequently is seen as a light-skinned person of color, or as white. Some have viewed this as a negative, while others believe it is an example of the loa manifesting in all shapes and races. I will let you draw your own conclusions. I do, however, find it interesting that for many loa and orisha, statuary comes in a full range of skin tones.

At her core, La Sirene is both mystery and mastery. According to some, it is she who takes departed souls under the water to the afterlife. Her sacred body sings of love, beauty, and the promise of something better. She is frequently seen as an initiator, bringing individuals into the religion of Haitian Vodou. She is also present in New Orleans Voodoo practices, where her role is that of a siren warning of danger, and cautioning of possible pitfalls.

La Sirene in Art and Creation

The supreme beauty of La Sirene makes her a favored subject in artwork. She is seen on ritual flags or drapo, frequently beaded in her colors of blue and white. The most common image of her is that of a mermaid, accompanied by the loa Agwe in the form of a boat. Together they can navigate even the most difficult waters. The Catholic lithographs most often used to represent her are Caridad del Cobre, Santa Marta, Stella Maris, or just Mary. Ritual flags also feature fish, horns, anchors, and other items. In many ways, it is almost as if the watery face of this loa is always changing, like the sea itself.

One particular dance done to honor La Sirene is the Parigol. It features swaying hip movements and an undulating movement similar, but less grandiose, than those featured in the Yanvalou. The dancers move their skirts and arms in waves to mimic the movement of the sea. An amazing version of the Parigol rhythm is featured on the *Drums of Vodou* recording released by Frisner Augustin in 1994. Augustin was a master drummer and an integral part of La Troupe Makandal, an Afro-Haitian music and dance company that was founded in 1973 and is still in operation today in Brooklyn, New York.

La Sirene Offerings

Offerings for La Sirene are customarily left at the sea, and include the following:

- Cake
- Champagne
- Combs
- Gin
- Honey
- Jordan almonds
- Melon
- Mirror
- Molasses
- Rice pudding
- Shells
- White rum

Workings for La Sirene

You may wish to perform a working for La Sirene when things seem particularly unclear.

SETTING A TABLE FOR LA SIRENE

Creating a table or shrine for La Sirene can help you to connect with her watery divine energy.

Components

- Blue cloth
- Veve or another image for La Sirene
- Blue candle
- Comb
- Ocean water
- Seashells
- White or blue flowers

Make sure your ritual space is clean and cover it with the blue cloth. Place the veve or image of La Sirene in the center of the space. Put the candle on top of this. Then place the rest of the offerings around the table. Light the candle. As always, never leave a burning candle unattended. If necessary, extinguish it and relight it when you are able. ■

LA SIRENE RITUAL BATH

This bath is best prepared and used during the full moon. It will help to align your energy with the spirit of La Sirene and open you up to special blessings and opportunity.

Ingredients

- 1 cup ocean water
- 1 cup spring water
- 1 teaspoon indigo powder
- 3 drops honey

Gather all ingredients on your working altar or ritual table. Add the waters to a large glass jar. Next add the indigo and honey, and shake well. Sing a song or play a sacred sound for La Sirene. (Some practitioners honor her with the sound made when blowing a conch shell.) Now the mixture is ready for use in your ritual bath. Add ½ cup or more to your bathwater as needed. ■

Ayizan

Ayizan is most often seen as the loa who is customarily assigned to the mambo (priestess) of a Haitian Vodou temple. She guides and protects these spiritual mothers of the hounfor. Some practitioners believe she is the wife of the loa Papa Legba, the owner of the crossroads. Others see her as the bride of Papa Loko, the loa who is often associated with the houngan (priest) of the temple. However, she has other allies as well. In her works Ayizan is frequently assisted by the loas Damballa and Sobo. She is seen as part of the Rada nation of loas.

As with many of the loas and orishas discussed in this book, there are many different manifestations of Ayizan. One of the most well known is Ayizan Velekete, but there is also Ayizan Loko, Gran Ayizan, Ayizan Belekounde, and Ayizan Poumgwe, to name just a few.

Ayizan is viewed as presiding over the initiation rites and rituals of Haitian Vodou. These most frequently begin with the *lavé tet* ceremony, a spiritual baptism which is her domain. Initiation is a vital step for anyone seriously interested in African traditional religions such as Haitian Vodou or New Orleans Voodoo. The lavé tet is designed to bring clarity and direction. The ceremony allows an individual to be seen and recognized by the loa. It affords them a deep cleansing, which bestows clarity and a new beginning. Ayizan represents the great benefits and knowledge that can be had through the process of initiation. Ayizan may be considered the first mambo of Vodou. Because of this, she is one of the first loa honored during ceremonies. A typical order of service might be a salute to Papa Legba, then the divine twins known as the Marassa, then Ayizan and Papa Loko. The color most often associated with Ayizan is white, but certain houses also use silver or gold in connection with her.

The name Ayizan is often interpreted as meaning from the earth or land, and this strengthens the basis for her connection to sacred plants and locations. Many see her as a loa deeply in touch with herbal medicines and magick. She rules over the marketplace and all the commerce and dealings that can take place there. In this area, she provides protection and insight for those who walk there. She knows how to make deals and find the best price, and is often turned to when devotees travel in this arena.

While primarily associated with Haitian Vodou, she is present in New Orleans Voodoo practices as well. Some even connect her to the great Voodoo queen Marie Laveau, and there is evidence that practices honoring her there date back hundreds of years. She is given a prominent place at the Voodoo Spiritual Temple, where I practice, and parts of her ritual veve are even incorporated into the temple's original logo.

Ayizan in Art and Music

Ayizan is often represented in Haitian ritual art via drapo and veves. The most common veve for Ayizan is a right-side-up V with curling ends on both sides, and an upside-down V with curling ends on top. It also features horizontal lines throughout. This design is similar to the veve for the Marassa, the divine twins, and also may bear some resemblance to the Masonic symbol, depending on how far you want to stretch your imagination. Some see this element of the veve as representative of her cosmic duality, and some have even envisioned her as gender-fluid, surpassing the boundaries of both these realms. As I have mentioned, individual veves are often combined to make larger creations. In this vein, the veve for Ayizan is frequently pictured with the veve for her husband Papa Loko. Together they form the support, or basis, for the spiritual family. She is also depicted with her veve surrounded by the sacred serpents Damballa and Aida Wedo, who are known to travel with her when there is important work to be done.

Ayizan is also represented by the image of St. Clare, who was said to have referred to herself as "the little plant." This loa's connection to plants can be seen as a partial reason for this association. Artist depictions often show Ayizan with her face covered, either with palm fronds or a veil of beads. Her rites, and even her face, are ever shrouded in mystery. In some spiritual houses the loas themselves are referred to as *les mysteres,* and Ayizan is the mistress of these mysteries.

There are many traditional songs for Ayizan. Many call out to her in song for her assistance with healing or solving disputes. Some of the songs tell of her searching, but also illustrate that she finds everything she needs in the end. The popular Haitian musical group RAM featured a song for Ayizan on their *RAM II: Puritan Vodou* recording released in 1997. Other artists such as the amazing Paul Beaubrun, Mizik Mizik, Jude Jean, Wesli, Francilia, and others have also recorded musical tracks dedicated to her. Her abilities are legendary, and it is easy to see why so many have chosen to honor her in this creative way.

Ayizan Offerings

Offerings to Ayizan are frequently left out in nature and placed upon palm fronds. These are also sometimes hung from the ceiling or roof during ceremonies to protect and consecrate the space. Many collect palm fronds when they are given out by the Catholic Church on Palm Sunday to use for her. Unlike many of the other loas, she is seen by many followers to not take alcohol of any kind. Here are a few of her popular offerings:

- Candy
- Dirt from the marketplace crossroads
- Mirliton or chayote squash
- Palm fronds
- Plantains
- Rocks gathered from the mountains
- White flowers
- Yams

Ayizan Workings

Ayizan workings and offerings are particularly helpful when you are going through initiations or changes in your life.

STUFFED MIRLITON OR CHAYOTE SQUASH

This is a popular dish in New Orleans and the Caribbean. Squash is one of the few foods given to Ayizan in ritual, and this can be made for feasts or ceremonies honoring Ayizan and the powerful ancestral foremothers of the African traditional religions. Feel free to add your own personal touches—add meat or seafood, or make a vegetarian version if you so desire. This particular take on things includes pork sausage.

Ingredients

- 3 medium mirliton or chayote squash (about 2 ½ pounds)
- 2 tablespoons butter
- 1 cup red onion, chopped
- 1 celery stalk, chopped
- ½ cup green pepper, chopped
- ½ cup red pepper, chopped
- 1 tablespoon minced garlic
- ½ pound cooked and chopped sausage
- 3 tablespoons parsley, chopped
- 2 tablespoons basil, chopped
- 2 tablespoons sage, chopped
- 1 tablespoon thyme, chopped
- ¾ cup toasted breadcrumbs
- 1 egg, beaten
- Salt and pepper to taste

Place whole squash in a large saucepan, cover with water, and boil. Depending on the size of the squash, you may need to boil for 30 to 45 minutes until fork tender. Remove squash from the water and set aside to cool completely. Split in half, remove seeds, and scoop out the pulp from the shell. Set both the shells and pulp aside until later.

Preheat oven to 350 degrees. Melt the butter over low heat in a frying pan. Add the onions and cook until they begin to become translucent. Add celery, red and green pepper, and garlic. Stir frequently for 3 or 4 minutes or until peppers begin to soften. Then add the reserved squash pulp, sausage, parsley, basil, sage, and thyme. Cook for 5 to 6 minutes more over low heat. Remove from the stove, stir in breadcrumbs, egg, and add salt and pepper to taste. Gently fill the squash shells with the stuffing mixture, dividing it equally between the halves. Bake in preheated oven for 15 or 20 minutes. Serves 6. ■

CANDLE FOR AYIZAN

Many people often come to me looking for advice in finding a teacher or elder to guide them on their path. Now, while not everyone is called to initiate fully on every level, in my opinion almost everyone who is serious about becoming connected to the religion can benefit from a head washing or lavé tet. In addition to the actual work of asking people, getting psychic readings, going to ceremonies, and seeking a teacher through traditional means, individuals seeking this path may benefit from leaving an offering or lighting a candle like this one for Ayizan.

Ingredients

- White cloth
- White flour, for veve for Ayizan
- Palm fronds
- White candle (or one with an image of Ayizan)
- 1 yam
- Dried peppermint or herbal tea

To start, make sure you complete this working in silence—try to keep outside noise to a minimum. Assemble all ingredients on your working altar or ritual space. Place the white cloth down. You may choose to draw the veve for Ayizan in white flour, or on a piece of parchment paper. While you are creating it, think about the transformational power of baptism and initiation. Concentrate on how you hope to see these desires manifesting for yourself. When the veve is completed, arrange the palm fronds and then place the candle on top of them. Place the yam in front of the candle. Play some music for Ayizan and light the candle. After it has been burning for a while, add a small pinch of peppermint or tea to the melting candle wax. Sprinkle the rest of the peppermint/tea over the yam. Allow the candle to burn down.

When the candle has burned down, gather all the remains of the working and bring them to nature. Anything that is biodegradable should be placed under a large tree in order to return to the earth. The other items can be recycled or disposed of accordingly. ■

In her role as the archetypal priestess Ayizan almost transcends time. She helps individuals navigate through time and space, doing so with great wisdom and oftentimes profound silence. She represents purity of intent and guidance on many levels. Despite her age, she is still known to help intercede on behalf of her followers. She holds a special power for female devotees. She and her partner, Papa Loko, are seen as not only spiritual parents of initiates to the tradition, but of the entire religion itself. Her maternal energy brings peace and protection to the whole community.

10

ANNIE CHRISTMAS AND MAMAN BRIGITTE: NEW-WORLD STRENGTH AND CONFIDENCE

People like to say that there are an infinite number of loas. I've heard the number referred to as 401, 1001, which means as many as you can think of and then add an extra just in case. This is because everyone has the ability to become elevated and honored after they have passed. The religions of Haitian Vodou and New Orleans Voodoo, as I have discussed, are fluid to some extent, and new elements are very often incorporated as necessary. This is the case with the loas Maman Brigitte and Annie Christmas. They arose because of circumstance and of deep need.

Annie Christmas

In the case of Annie Christmas in New Orleans, many believe she was an actual person. There are many tales and stories telling of her legendary life. She was said to have been striking, with dark skin, standing over 7 feet tall, and weighing over 250 pounds. Annie Christmas was either a steamboat captain or a railroad worker, depending on which story you are hearing. Called the "biggest woman in Louisiana," she had several sons, and her great strength was known throughout the world. Some versions of her story say she fell in love with a steamboat captain, while others say that Keelboat Annie, as she is also called, either never married or was a widow for most of her life.

It's easy to see why she is still talked about today; she could beat up any man, and she often served up some justice to local bullies and thugs. After each beatdown, she was said to add a new pearl to her necklace, which was believed to hold her power.

The most popular part of her story explains how she saved hundreds of people from drowning on the Mississippi. It begins with a foolish captain leading a steamboat down the river in a raging storm. He makes one wrong turn after another, despite Annie trying to advise him how to navigate the difficulties. In the end, it is Annie who rescues the people on the boat with her wit and skill. Some variations talk about how she steered the perilous boat herself, while others have her making the rescue with her own keelboat. In any case, she saved the day.

The world of New Orleans Voodoo today still honors Annie Christmas as one of the foremothers of the city. Because of her character she is seen as a kind of female Ogun, displaying masculine strength and power despite her given gender. It is said that "no one can tame Annie Christmas, and no one can tame the Mississippi."

Offerings for Annie Christmas

The following offerings are usually brought to the riverside, or at least the water's edge. Altars and shrines for Annie Christmas are almost nonexistent, but maybe as time passes this too will change.

- Black candle
- Dark rum
- Iron chains
- Pearls
- River water
- Rue
- Sassafras
- Small boats

Workings for Annie Christmas

Annie Christmas reminds us of our own inner strength and power. Use these workings to get in touch with your own strength, and to find out how you can help others who may be subjectd to unfair treatment.

ANNIE CHRISTMAS GRIS-GRIS BAG

This bag is to be carried with you at all times. It will help bring you strength and victory over your enemies.

Ingredients

- Iron filings
- 1 tablespoon rue
- 1 tablespoon guinea pepper
- 1 pearl

Assemble your ingredients on your ritual altar or space. Add all ingredients to a small natural cloth bag and tie it shut. Throw the bag gently in the air to bless it with the energy of the world of the invisibles. Catch the bag with both hands. Carry the bag to remember and honor the strength, courage, and ingenuity of Annie Christmas. ■

ANNIE CHRISTMAS FLOOR WASH

This floor wash is used to fortify and bless your space with the Ashe or energy of Annie Christmas.

Ingredients

- 1 cup river water
- 2 cups spring water

- Pinch of sassafras (file powder)
- 3 drops sandalwood
- 1 piece lodestone

Place a large glass or ceramic bowl in the center of your ritual space or altar. Add the waters, sassafras, and sandalwood. Stir counterclockwise. Then add the lodestone. Use the wash to wipe down your threshold, windows, and corners to fill your home with security and protective forces. When you are finished, dump the leftover water out at a crossroads or near the railroad tracks if possible. ■

Maman Brigitte

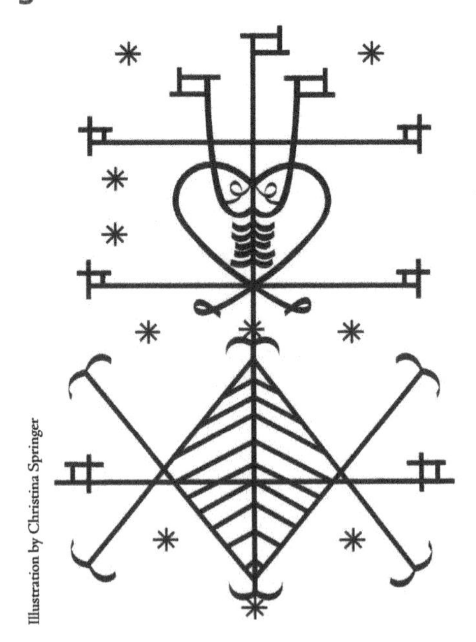

Illustration by Christina Springer

There is a dark mistress of the cemetery, a bride dressed in white lace. She knows of love and loss, and her name is Maman Brigitte. In the religions of New Orleans Voodoo and Haitian Vodou, Maman Brigitte, also called Gran Brigitte or Manman Brijit, is the loa of the dead. She is honored as the first woman buried in each cemetery. To leave offerings for her, seek out this oldest grave and commune with the ancient wisdom you find there.

She is known by some to be the wife of the Baron Samedi, most famous for his top hat and beguiling smile. Alongside her husband, Maman Brigitte guides and protects those who seek her blessing. Here devotees can find wisdom, connection, and healing justice.

The first time I met Maman Brigitte in person was at a ritual given by one of the larger Haitian Vodou houses in Philadelphia. The tables were set with purple lace cloths, purple candles, and small bowls of cigarettes. It was clear we were entering the realm of the dead. The ceremony began with drumming and dancing, and as the evening progressed several members of the hounfor became graced with the energy of Maman Brigitte. They dressed in all their ritual finery—expensive jewelry, furs, and sequins were everywhere. They then went among the congregation offering blessings, wisdom, and playful guidance. They urged to be realistic about life, but also to have a good sense of humor. Like the legion of ancestral foremothers she represents, Maman Brigitte urges us to examine our hopes and desires, as well as our actions.

Art for Maman Brigitte

Maybe because of her striking image, Maman Brigitte is frequently the subject of art in Haitian Vodou. Firstly, there are the veves that are found throughout the religion. The most popular one depicts a heart issuing forth from a tombstone. There is both a fierceness and a gravity to the images depicting Maman Brigitte. She has found a place in many modern artists' conceptions because the image of a dead bride is compelling and powerful.

Very often she is given a skeleton face and a bridal gown in portraits and artistic representations. Her primary colors, black and purple, are also prominent. She is also depicted wearing a veil or a large black top hat, like the one worn by the Barons. Here in Brooklyn, several organizations and spiritual houses have chosen to honor Maman Brigitte with costume parties and celebrations where participants will dress as the loa. The gatherings are a beautiful expression of all that Maman Brigitte has come to represent. There is certainly an aspect of Maman Brigitte that lends herself to these physical transformations, just as death itself is a physical transformation.

Here in our own spiritual house, we often honor her creatively by making Maman Brigitte ancestor jars. These are filled with sacred dirt of the cemeteries or, even better, graves of our honored ancestors. These are elaborately decorated with beads, shells, sequins, fine lace, and fabric. One of the things that creating these jars helps us to do is connect with their sacred energy, or Ashe, even when we may be far away from their physical graves.

I had the supreme pleasure some years ago of attending a lecture by Alejandro Jodorowsky, author, filmmaker, tarot reader, and magician. During his talk, one of the ladies in the audience told him that she felt disconnected from her ancestors and foremothers, and asked how she might establish a better relationship with them. His answer was immediate. The solution was, she should cover herself with the dirt of her homeland. If that land was far away, she should do her best to find a way to import some. For some, this may sound extreme; but connecting with the actual dirt from where your ancestors lay is very powerful.

I had a woman come to me once for a psychic reading. She was wishing to connect with her ancestors from several generations back in Ethiopia, despite the fact that her family had lived in the United States for several decades. Normally, I would have suggested she make a jar for Maman Brigitte and her ancestors with the dirt from their graves. But we were thousands of miles from Ethiopia, and I wondered how this could be possible. Then, toward the end of her reading, I remembered that a dear friend had brought me some dirt from Ethiopia almost a decade before. I quickly produced it for her. It's amazing how the universe provides solutions sometimes even before it reveals the questions.

In accordance with Maman Brigitte's connection to the Irish saint, some people use the image of St. Brigit of Kildare to represent her.

In addition to visual art, Maman Brigitte is also honored with dance. Here in New York City I have been blessed to study with Haitian Dance Master Teacher Julio Jean. Jean is a renowned teacher and choreographer with over twenty years of experience. He blends traditional Haitian forms with modern and contemporary dance to create compelling movement narratives. As a teacher, he pays great attention to detail while bringing forth the powerful beauty of the dances. The dances for Maman Brigitte, the Barons, and the Gede are very lusty and sexual. Many of the movements are low to the ground, and sensual teasing and grinding hips are prevalent. Props are often part of these dances too, with participants using hats, canes, and glasses to tell their artful story.

Offerings for Maman Brigitte

The following offerings can be left at the cemetery or on your ancestor shrine to help you connect with the Ashe of Maman Brigitte.

- Beets
- Chili peppers
- Cigarettes
- Coffee
- Cornmeal
- Cotton
- Elm bark
- High John root
- Irish moss
- Red wine
- Rum
- Nanny goat
- Oranges
- Peanuts
- Sweet potatoes
- Willow bark

Maman Brigitte Workings

As a mighty foremother Maman Brigitte is one of the loa you may wish to connect with through workings and rituals. These will help you to connect with this ancient and powerful energy,

MAMAN BRIGITTE CAIRN

The most common shrine built for Maman Brigitte isn't a traditional-looking one; instead, it is a cairn. A cairn is a manmade pile of stones that is used as a marker, most often a grave marker. They are primarily found in Celtic countries, and the word itself is derived from Scottish Gaelic. You may choose to create your cairn in the cemetery or at the base of an elm or willow tree, as both are sacred to her.

Ingredients

- 1 tablespoon coffee
- 3 cotton balls
- Several small stones
- Small white candle

Gather all your ingredients. With the coffee, make a small circle on the earth where you are going to build your cairn. Next, place the cotton balls in the center of the circle. Make a circle around this with the stones. Place layer upon layer of stones going up in a circle until your creation has reached your desired size. It may take some practice balancing the stones in the right way.

When you are finished, place the candle in front of the cairn and light it. As it burns, express respect for Maman Brigitte and all the mothers who have come before. Tell her of the injustices and disputes that you are involved in. Listen silently for her wise solutions and guidance. As always, never leave a burning candle unattended. ■

MAMAN BRIGITTE CANDLE

This is a great candle to use if you are trying to connect with your female ancestors and the dead. They can bring solutions for everyday problems.

Ingredients

- 7-day candle in glass, either purple or with an image of Maman Brigitte
- Cotton balls
- Cemetery water
- 3 drops violet oil
- 3 drops heliotrope oil
- 3 drops lavender oil
- Old coins

Place the candle securely in a bowl and surround it with the cotton and the coins. Pour a small amount of water on the cotton balls to dampen them. Add the oils to the top of the candle and light it.

Many of Maman Brigitte's messages come in silence, so sit quietly and do your best to hear what she is saying. Do not leave a burning candle unattended, but instead put it out every night and repeat the process until the candle has burned down. ■

MAMAN BRIGITTE OIL

This ritual oil is designed to honor this first mistress of the cemetery. You can wear it or use it as an offering when you wish to receive information or messages from the dead.

Ingredients

- ½ ounce sweet almond oil
- 3 drops lilac oil

- 3 drops myrrh oil
- 3 drops orange oil

Place the almond oil into a small glass bottle. Add the other oils one at a time. Rub the oil quickly between your hands to charge it. Then it is ready for use. ■

MAMAN BRIGITTE GRIS-GRIS

Carry this gris-gris when you are facing injustice.

Ingredients

- Natural cotton balls
- ¼ cup dried orange peel
- ¼ cup dried violets
- 1 teaspoon cemetery dirt
- 3 drops frankincense

Place the cotton balls, orange peel, violets, cemetery dirt, and frankincense into a glass jar. Shake well to combine. If you can, bury the jar overnight to charge it with the powers of earth. If that is not possible, get yourself a bucket and a bag of potting soil and cover it that way, disposing of the extra dirt at the base of a large tree when you are finished with the working. Uncover the jar and place the contents inside a purple bag. ■

Maman Brigitte in some ways represents the ancient mother archetype. I have met some worshipers who associate Maman Brigitte with the Celtic deity Brigid and call upon her healing powers. New Orleans had an influx of Irish workers in its beginnings, and some blending has been suggested. You will, however, need to understand the similarities and differences between Maman Brigitte and Brigid if you choose to welcome both of these energies into your life. While her inclusion here may seem puzzling to some, there is a long history of connection between Celtic and

African culture. While the original blending of Maman Brigitte and Brigid occurred centuries ago, there are still many who honor them separately or together today. In the interest of clarity I have included some information about Brigid here.

Brigid

Brigid is one of the most well-known goddesses in the Celtic pantheon. This is a goddess of many names and many places. She is also called Brigit, Brighid, Bride, Breeshey, Brigh, and Brigantia, and is even associated with St. Brigit, who, along with St. Patrick, is honored as one of the patron saints of Ireland. Brigid translates to "fiery one" or "bright arrow" in the ancient language of the Celts, referring to her connections to the sun and sacred flame. She is, however, also paradoxically associated with healing water.

There are in excess of fifteen sacred wells in Ireland dedicated to Brigid, with the most famous being the one near the Cliffs of Moher in County Clare. This sacred healing well has been the site of pilgrimages for hundreds of years. It is in a sacred grotto that serves as a gateway to the nearby cemetery. The well and the water within it are said to possess great healing powers. This is a liminal place, a site of magick and mystery. If you have the chance to visit, I highly recommend it.

While both fire and water are Brigid's domain, she is also the patron deity of prophecy, the hearth, poets, midwives, healers, sailors, travelers, and fugitives. Many animals are also said to fall under her protection, particularly snakes, lambs, bees, cows, and owls.

Herbs and Offerings for Brigid

Brigid offerings can be left at sacred wells or burnt in ritual fires. You may also choose to just leave them on your altar or shrine as part of a larger working.

- Angelica
- Basil
- Blackberry
- Chamomile
- Clover
- Dandelion
- Dill
- Hazel
- Heather
- Heliotrope
- Hops
- Irish moss
- Lavender
- Myrrh
- Oak
- Primrose
- Rosemary
- Rowan
- Violet
- Willow
- Wisteria

BRIGID RITUAL BATH

A goddess of sacred healing water obviously lends her talents when creating a magickal bath. Since her well is especially venerated during Lughnasadh, the summer harvest festival celebrated on August 1, this would be an ideal time for making and taking this bath. However, the healing powers of Brigid are available whenever needed, so feel free to use this at other times of the year as well.

Ingredients

- 1 quart spring water
- 1 cup holy water
- Handful of violet blossoms
- Handful of chamomile blossoms
- Sprig of fresh rosemary

Assemble all ingredients on your shrine or working ritual altar. Fill a bowl with spring water. Take the bowl outside and pour the water out onto the open earth. Bring the bowl back inside. Then fill the bowl with holy water, flower blossoms, and rosemary. Raise the bowl up high above your head, and then lower it down to gently touch the ground. Pour the contents of the bowl into a bottle along with the remaining spring water. Place outside on your windowsill for a full day where the rays of both the sun and the moon will touch and bless it. Now it is ready to strain and use in your bath. Pour the entire mixture into your tub and then fill with warm water. Get in and focus your energy and intent on bringing healing to you and your environment. ■

BRIGID PROPHECY SPELL

Since Brigid is known as a goddess of sacred prophecy, it makes logical sense that she is honored in spellwork designed to bring insight from the divine. This spell combines two of her ritual elements—water and fire—to help bless and charge your divination tools. These tools are vitally important for helping guide you in your spiritual growth. Every individual is unique, and these tools will help you find the proper steps to make on your own sacred journey.

Ingredients

- Spring water
- 3 drops lavender oil
- 3 drops myrrh oil
- Pinch of dill
- Pinch of dried chamomile flowers
- Small red candle
- Divination item (tarot cards, pendulum, dowsing rods, etc.)
- Small piece of moonstone

Gather all of your items on a white cloth. Place a glass bowl in the center of the cloth and fill it halfway with spring water. Add the lavender, myrrh, dill, and chamomile. Then place the red candle into a holder and situate it in the center of the water bowl. Place your divination item on the cloth in between yourself and the bowl. As you light the candle, say the following blessing, or one of your own choosing:

> Sacred Water, Sacred Flame, please bless these tools in your
> Sacred Name.
> (Repeat three times.)

If possible, leave the candle burning in front of your divination tools until it is done. You may now use your divination tools again. They have been refreshed and blessed by the goddess, so please treat them accordingly. Try not to place them directly on the ground, and be mindful of who you let touch them. ■

BRIGID LAVENDER HONEY

The hearth has always been regarded as the magickal center of a home. While not many of us have a central hearth fire used for both cooking and warmth anymore, we still do have a place for cooking and preparing the food that sustains us. Since Brigid is the goddess of the hearth, it seems only fitting that I invoke my own kitchen witch nature here and provide you with some recipes to nourish and sustain you and your loved ones. The following is one of my favorite magickal recipes. It can be used to bring healing, happiness, insight, and other blessings. The ideal time to prepare it is Imbolc or February 2, when she is honored in most Celtic countries.

Ingredients

- 1 cup clover honey
- 3 tablespoons organic dried lavender blossoms

Heat the honey in a small saucepan over very low heat. Add the lavender and stir with a wooden spoon counterclockwise three times, then clockwise three times. Cover and remove from heat. Let the covered mixture settle and infuse overnight.

The next day, place the pan over low heat. Warm slightly; then strain honey through a cheesecloth into a glass jar. Honey can be refrigerated for up to six months, but serve at room temperature. Makes a delightful addition to tea and biscuits or scones. ■

BRIGID OATCAKES

Being a harvest goddess, Brigid is often celebrated with oats. Both physically and spiritually, oats are known to bring joy and battle depression. You can make them as an offering to the goddess and for yourself on Imbolc, or anytime you need a little boost. I love that this recipe includes botanicals to honor Brigid's true nature. They always remind me that spring and summer are coming no matter how dark and cold the day may seem. It is worthy to note that Brigid is seen as the daughter of the goddess Boyne. She rules the river Boyne near Brú na Bóinne in County Meath, Ireland. It is here that ancient tombs align themselves with the light of the solstice, providing illumination and insight. Craft this recipe when you need guidance and shining hope in your own life.

Ingredients

- 2 cups old-fashioned oats
- 1 cup sour milk or buttermilk
- 2 ¼ cups flour, sifted
- 1 teaspoon baking powder
- ½ teaspoon baking soda
- 1 teaspoon salt
- 1 teaspoon dried lavender blossoms, crushed
- 1 teaspoon dried chamomile blossoms, crushed
- 1 teaspoon dried violet blossoms, crushed
- Jam and/or butter

Mix the oats and milk together. Cover, refrigerate, and let sit overnight. Take the oats out of the refrigerator and bring to room temperature. Preheat the oven to 350 degrees. Grease a cookie sheet with butter.
In a separate bowl, mix the flour, baking powder, baking soda, salt, and dried flowers thoroughly with a wooden spoon. Add the oats and milk mixture a little at a time, stirring well after each addition, until a dough forms.

Shape the dough into a large round, approximately 1 inch thick, and place it on the cookie sheet. Make a crossroads on the top with a knife. Bake for 30 minutes, or until the top is browned and a toothpick inserted near the center comes out clean. Cool and enjoy with the honey recipe given above, jam, and/or fresh butter. ■

Maman Brigitte is at her core a powerful protector. I have met some who call on her for justice, particularly important in this time of racial unrest. Whatever reason you might have to whisper her name, and smile humbly in her direction, the above spells and offerings will help to honor your connection to her and to the ancestors, providing protection and great blessings.

11

MARIE LAVEAU AND THE VOODOO QUEENS

A Voodoo queen is a woman who holds the power and majesty of the religion of Voodoo. Undoubtedly, the most famous Voodoo queen of all time is Marie Laveau. Her grave at St. Louis Cemetery Number One is the second most popular gravesite in the United States, after Elvis Presley. Today people take guided tours, leave devotional offerings, and make the sacred pilgrimage to hear her story. Unfortunately, some of the information circulating about her over the years has been sketchy at best. There are, however, some references to this Voodoo queen in the work of Zora Neale Hurston and in the Louisiana Writers' Project.

Born in 1794 or 1801, depending on which source is consulted, Marie Laveau is described as a woman of beauty, grace, entrepreneurship, psychic power, and great skill. Marie Laveau's maternal grandmother is believed to have been a free woman of color named Catherine, a New Orleans native born in the 1750s. Catherine was originally born into slavery, as were her four children, including Marie Laveau's mother, Marguerite, who is listed in government records as a "mulatto," which is today referred to as biracial. Marie married Jacques Paris in 1819, but he disappeared early into their marriage. For most of her life, Marie Laveau was called the Widow Paris. She did manage to give birth to several children with her life partner, Christophe Glapion. Some say she had fifteen children, though records remain for only seven. At least one of these was named Marie. Part of the confusion about many of the details of her life stem from the fact that her daughter Marie assumed many of her spiritual duties as the original Marie grew older.

The legacy of Marie Laveau lives on in the modern-day queens that grace the magickal city of New Orleans. The landscape of the religion has changed in recent years, and now you can find Voodoo on almost every corner; Marie Laveau's House of Voodoo at 739 Bourbon Street is filled with magickal products, altars, and psychics. Her legacy is alive and vibrant. One of my favorite stories about Marie Laveau happened during a time when individuals were still able to access the tomb of Marie Laveau without a tour guide. My dear friend Witchdoctor Utu and I had traveled a long way to see the grave of the Voodoo queen and leave offerings as well as perform a small ceremony with drumming and dancing. We left our gifts and began our rite, and about halfway through we gained an audience. A tour group had come through with a less than fully informed guide. The thing about Marie Laveau is that she is so widely known that almost everyone considers themselves an expert. The guide began to tell the crowd that had gathered that we were a "supposed Voodoo ritual." She doubted our validity because, well, "Voodoo doesn't happen during the day." Honestly, it was all we could do to keep from laughing. Obviously, Voodoo happens whenever and wherever it needs to. It is a powerful, ancient religion that refused to be squashed no matter what difficulties were thrown at it.

In recent years, much scholarship, and even popular media, has been centered on Marie Laveau. She was indeed larger than life, and in many ways larger than death too. She was a mother, a businesswoman, and a priestess. Laveau was the first woman to perform open ceremonies in the city. These rites took place at Congo Square, the Bayou St. John, and Lake Pontchartrain. It is said these were attended by people of all races and classes. Part of her rise to power is due to the fact that she traveled through many different social and professional circles. Originally working as a hairdresser, she was afforded access to and leverage with some of the most influential people in New Orleans. She used all she could to survive and thrive.

Manifestations of Marie Laveau

Many artists and followers have chosen to draw, paint, or connect with Marie Laveau through art. By far the most well-known image of her is the painting that hangs in the museum at the Cabildo in Jackson Square. Jackson Square is the place where readers gather today to foretell the future just as Marie did. Another portrait hangs in the New Orleans Voodoo Museum. This one was created by the founder of the museum, the late Charles Gandolfo. This image was based on one created by an artist named G. William Nott and appeared in the November 19, 1922, issue of the *Times-Picayune*. All of these representations exist despite the fact that Marie's daughter Philomene told a reporter that Marie never sat for a photo or portrait.

Even if we may never know for certain what the face of Marie Laveau looked like, we may be able to connect with her energy, her Ashe, which lingers on in the New Orleans air like the delightful scent of jasmine or magnolia. As for artwork, Marie Laveau is featured in addition to traditional portraits, in detailed veves, or ritual ground drawings. Most of the veves for her incorporate a heart, and sometimes her initials M and L. Some believe that the heart is designed to represent her connection to Erzulie, the Haitian loa. Other veves feature a snake; this is representative of her connection to the sacred serpents Damballa and Aida Wedo, and also of her own snake Simbi, which she was said to place on her head like a royal crown. There is even a restaurant in Spain which features a Marie Laveau veve adorned with alligators.

Numerous songs, books, and stories have been created about this famous Voodoo queen. One of the most popular is the Shel Silverstein song that calls her the most famous of all the Voodoo queens. Then there is the Marie Laveau song originally popularized by Papa Celestin, and later sung by the late Jazz legend Dr. John, who I was proud to call a friend. Some of the lyrics on his album *N'awlinz: Dis Dat Or D'udda* (2004) say that she sure knows how to put that Voodoo down.

People don't only sing about Marie Laveau; they paint pictures of her, and even feature her as a main character in their television series, as was the case with *American Horror Story*. This show cast Angela Bassett as the Voodoo queen, and in keeping with the horror theme, exaggerated and sensationalized much of Laveau's talents and history. I can't say that I was surprised with the history Hollywood has of maligning the religion. It is my hope that with this book and others people will discover the real history for themselves, which is much stranger and more colorful than even the wildest of Hollywood's producers could imagine. The real Laveau stood for justice for the oppressed and was known for her charitable works benefiting the less fortunate. Some interviews even tell us that she allowed some of the indigenous Choctaw women to set up camp on her property on St. Ann Street. Others report that her home with Glapion may have been a secret stop on the Underground Railroad. Unfortunately, that is not what gets remembered about the famous Voodoo queen.

Marie Laveau was a spiritual leader to all who came to her, from former slaves to Queen Victoria. She used her skills and talents in the best ways possible. In *Mules and Men*, Zora Neale Hurston tells us that Laveau could turn the police on themselves, making them bark, run, and attack each other. In all aspects Marie Laveau shows us the values of resourcefulness, compassion, and feminine power.

There were other Voodoo queens in New Orleans before Marie Laveau, women with exotic names like Sanite Dede and Marie Saloppe. Many of these were free women of color who helped to define the religion in the city's early days. Many of the Voodoo practices were forced to take place in secret, as there were laws forbidding public drumming and dancing. These prohibitions were not just limited to New Orleans.

There were spiritual queens in other places too, like back in Africa. One of the most famous was the amazing and fierce African queen Nzinga. Nzinga was named according to tradition because at birth her umbilical cord was wrapped around her neck (the Kimbundu verb *kujinga* means to twist). This is said to mean the person would be proud. She lived up to her name, becoming a visionary and a foremother to modern warrior women everywhere. She was born in 1582 as Nzinga Mbande Ngola and is known as Africa's "Joan of Arc." From the very start, Nzinga fought against involvement in her native land of Ndongo, later renamed Angola. Popular legend says she had a harem of over sixty men for her sensual pleasure, putting them to death after a single sexual encounter. She was known for her skill with weaponry, and it was said she carried a sharpened machete onto the battlefield. She is still honored today, most notably with a statue in Kinaxixi Square, Luanda, Angola.

Today, the universe of Voodoo in New Orleans is very different than it was in Marie Laveau's time. My own priestess Miriam Chamani has owned and operated the Voodoo Spiritual Temple in New Orleans for almost three decades. She is a truly powerful Voodoo queen in her own right. She started the temple with the late, great priest Oswan Chamani in 1990, and ever since it has served as a beacon for those who seek the truth about the ancient religion of Voodoo. In my documentary about New Orleans Voodoo, *Bodies of Water* (2004), Priestess Miriam talks about the city's connection to the water and how Voodoo is almost defined by it. She explains that our bodies are mostly made up of water, and, being next to a powerful force like the Mississippi River, the religion in the city has taken on its own special flavor.

The most sacred day in New Orleans Voodoo is St. John's Eve. It is remembered as the time Marie Laveau performed blessings and miracles for her followers back in the nineteenth century. Not that long ago, it was my absolute pleasure to introduce Priestess Miriam to musician Dr. John (Mac Rebennack) and participate in a St. John's Eve ritual with them on the edge of the Mississippi. We sang, ate, and offered blessings to the sizable crowd that had gathered. Like most Voodoo ceremonies, it lasted for hours and there was much joy to be had.

There are also several other Voodoo queens who grace the streets of the Crescent City today. In many ways, Voodoo functions as a matriarchy and always has. The women always run the show. This is similar to Haitian Vodou, where many of the mambos hold the secrets and the power of the religion.

Marie Laveau Offerings

Marie Laveau offerings can be left at her tomb, or simply at a crossroads whenever you wish to connect with the sacred energy of this Voodoo legend.

- Apples
- Blue candles
- Combs
- Holy water
- Jambalaya
- Jasmine
- Mirrors
- Oranges
- Red peppers
- Rice and beans
- Saltwater
- White candles
- White carnations

Workings for Marie Laveau

Understandably, many of us feel a connection and a kinship to Marie Laveau. Magickal workings to honor and strengthen these bonds are a positive way to manifest some of her great magick in our own lives.

MARIE LAVEAU SHRINE

People build shrines to Marie Laveau all over the world. One of the largest is the International Shrine of Marie Laveau at the New Orleans Healing Center. It was created by Mambo Sallie Ann Glassman as a place for visitors to leave offerings, petitions, and prayers. If you are unable to visit, you can create a Marie Laveau shrine of your own using the following instructions.

Components

- Image of Marie Laveau
- Comb
- Mirror
- 3 blue or purple candles, in holders
- 3 drops jasmine oil
- 3 drops lavender oil
- 3 drops magnolia oil
- Holy water (from a New Orleans church if possible)

Spread a blue or purple cloth out over your ritual space. Sprinkle it with the holy water. Place the image of Marie Laveau in the center of the space. Place the comb to the right of the image, and the mirror to the left of the image. Place a single candle in front of the Marie Laveau image, the mirror, and the comb. Put one drop of each oil on top of each candle. Light the candles. Your shrine is now set.

As the candles burn, the shrine will gain energy and power. Feel free to leave it up indefinitely, adding more candles and other offerings over time. It will be a great place to spiritually charge your tarot cards, runes, or other divination items, as well as your magickal jewelry. If you leave it up permanently, I recommend covering it with a white cloth when you are not actively using it. ■

MARIE LAVEAU HEALING WATER

This is one of my favorite formulas to create for Marie Laveau. It is used to heal your mind, body, and soul and create an atmosphere of lasting peace. One of my teachers likes to say that all spells and workings are in fact healing, because what you are trying to do is heal the problems in your life.

Ingredients

- Small purple candle
- Image of Marie Laveau
- Holy water from a Catholic church (preferably in New Orleans)
- Spring water
- Rose water
- Rain water
- 3 drops lavender oil
- 3 drops myrrh oil

Assemble all items on your ritual altar or working space. Light the candle in front of the image of Marie Laveau. Pour the waters and the oils into a small glass bottle. Rub the bottle between your hands as you focus on the image of Marie Laveau. It was said that Laveau was a devout Catholic throughout her life, so if you like, you may recite the following verses:

> Ask, and it shall be given you; seek, and ye
> shall find; knock, and it shall be opened unto you:
> For every one that asketh receiveth; and he that seeketh
> findeth; and to him that knocketh it shall be opened.
> (Matthew 7:7–8)

After you are done, take a long, deep breath and exhale it out onto the bottle to charge it with your own personal power. Sprinkle the water about your home, put it in your bath, or use it to wash your hands and feet. The Marie Laveau water will help to bring healing and peace to your life in all areas. ■

CRESCENT CITY GRIS-GRIS BAG

The energy of New Orleans is like no other. It holds a magick and a mystery all its own. It can be used to connect with Marie Laveau, Doctor John Montanee (Marie Laveau's high priest and drummer), Annie Christmas, or any of the other spiritual greats associated with the city.

Ingredients

- 3 teaspoons sassafras (file powder)
- 3 teaspoons lavender blossoms, dried
- 3 tonka beans
- 1 tablespoon shredded cypress bark
- 3 drops magnolia oil
- 3 drops oakmoss oil
- Small amethyst

Assemble all ingredients on your ritual altar or magickal space. Place the sassafras, lavender, tonka beans, and cypress in a glass bowl. Sprinkle with the oils and stir clockwise with a wooden spoon. Place the mixture into a small natural-fiber bag along with the amethyst crystal. Carry the bag in your pocket to help feel the power and blessings of New Orleans everywhere you go. ■

MARIE LAVEAU BOURBON BREAD PUDDING

Almost every restaurant in New Orleans has a bread pudding on the menu. The following is my own special recipe for the classic dish containing orange, lemon, and whiskey to give it that jazzy kick. It makes a perfect addition to your feast menu or for an offering.

Ingredients

Bourbon sauce:

- ¼ cup butter
- ¼ cup sugar
- ½ fresh vanilla bean
- 1 egg yolk, beaten
- 3 tablespoons bourbon
- 2 teaspoons grated lime peel
- 1 teaspoon grated lemon peel
- 2 tablespoons orange juice

Bread pudding:

- 4 slices sweet bread
- ⅓ cup cream cheese
- 1 ¾ cups light cream
- 3 eggs beaten
- ½ cup light brown sugar

Prepare the bourbon sauce:

Melt butter in saucepan on low heat. Add the sugar, vanilla bean, egg yolk, and 2 tablespoons water. Cook, stirring constantly, until all the sugar dissolves and mixture begins to boil, about 3 to 4 minutes. Remove from heat. Take out the vanilla bean, and stir in bourbon, citrus peels, and orange juice.

Prepare the bread pudding:

Preheat oven to 325 degrees. Spread the cream cheese on the bread to make two sandwiches. Cut each sandwich into 1-inch cubes and place in baking dish. Combine the cream and eggs, mix well, and pour over bread cubes. Bake for 40 minutes or until toothpick inserted into center of dish comes out clean. Remove from oven. Serve while slightly warm, covered with bourbon sauce and fresh whipped cream. ■

ST. JOHN'S EVE DELIGHT

As I mentioned earlier, the main holiday for New Orleans Voodoo and Marie Laveau is St. John's Eve. Here's a drink that I often use for St. John's Eve festivities. I hope you enjoy it. Drink on St. John's Eve or anytime to celebrate the spirit of the city.

Ingredients

- 1 ounce whiskey
- 1 teaspoon grenadine
- 4 ounces ginger ale
- Juice of 1 lime
- Lime wedge for garnish

Fill a cocktail shaker with ice and add all ingredients. Shake well. Pour into a glass over ice. Serves 1. ■

NEW ORLEANS VOODOO COFFEE

New Orleans Voodoo pairs its coffee with everything from blessings to bourbon. The magickal city is known for its preference for coffee with chicory. Chicory is said to impart the blessings of strength, luck, invisibility, and removal of obstacles. Natives of the Crescent City often add eggshells to cut the bitterness of the blend and give it a unique flavor all its own. The following recipe is dedicated to my good friends at the Voodoo Spiritual Temple in New Orleans and the coffeehouse Voobrew Café, which used to be next door to the temple's original location.

Ingredients

- 1 large cup dark roast coffee with chicory
- 1 healthy dash light cream
- Pinch of cinnamon
- Healthy dash of dark rum (preferably Barbancourt)
- ½ teaspoon vanilla extract
- 2 teaspoons cocoa powder

Mix all ingredients well in your favorite coffee cup and enjoy. ■

TEMPLE CREATION CORN

From my very beginnings as a part of the family at the Voodoo Spiritual Temple I was taught the importance of food. Many different traditions place an importance on the sacred power of food, and New Orleans Voodoo is no different. For me the food at a ceremony is just as vital, if not more so, than the other elements present. Food can be shared with everyone young and old, and great care should be taken to serve the best dishes possible. Over two decades ago, I learned this recipe and it has been one of my absolute favorites ever since.

Ingredients

- 1 tablespoon butter
- 1 can white corn kernels
- ¼ teaspoon onion powder
- ¼ teaspoon paprika
- 1 can creamed corn

- 2 tablespoons light cream
- Salt and pepper

Melt butter in a medium saucepan over low heat. Add white corn, onion powder, and paprika and stir. Next add the creamed corn. Simmer for 15 to 20 minutes, stirring frequently. Remove from heat. Add light cream and salt and pepper to taste. ■

Queen Nanny of Jamaica

Marie Laveau isn't the only powerful queen to grace the history of Voodoo and the other African traditional religions. Unfortunately, much of the recorded information was whitewashed and created by the patriarchy, and only some names have survived. One of these names was Queen Nanny, also known as Nanny of the Maroons. Nanny's name came from the word *nana,* a title of respect given to female elders of the Akan people in Africa.

Remembered as both a warrior and a queen, this woman was a powerful leader, and a force to be reckoned with. There are many differing reports of Nanny's life. Some recount that she was an escaped slave; some say she may have had slaves of her own. It is irrefutable, however, that she was a hero of Jamaica who very likely practiced that ancient African magick known as Obeah.

Many prefer to forget her connection to African healing methods and magick. Queen Nanny was said to have escaped her own captors and along with her brothers founded a free settlement in the Blue Mountains of Jamaica. From 1728 to 1740, Queen Nanny led what would later be referred to as the Windward Maroons. Under her command, they freed almost a thousand slaves over the years. She used her military skill along with her Obeah woman talents to successfully mount her campaigns. Some even believed she could work miracles.

One of her sacred sites is Nanny Falls in Portland, Jamaica. It is said the water here has great healing powers, and was visited by Nanny and her original warriors to fortify and test themselves before going into battle. She is also said to have owned a huge cauldron that was always kept boiling, despite the fact that it did not appear to be lit. There are tales that say this huge pot was placed at the end of the road near her camp and would lure soldiers close. Out of curiosity these soldiers would look into the pot and mysteriously fall in to their deaths. Some believe that this wasn't a cauldron at all, but a basin formed from rock in the Nanny River, which was always churning and appeared to be boiling up.

She is said to have worn the teeth of her enemies as jewelry. One of the most extreme legends about Queen Nanny says she had the ability to catch the bullets that were fired at her. Some say she caught them and returned fire by hurling them back. Others, probably influenced by an attempt to discredit her, said she caught these bullets in her behind and farted them back at the British soldiers with deadly precision.

Attitudes, stereotypes, and prejudices about Obeah are a holdover from a time not so long ago when these sacred practices were secret and vilified. I have traveled to Jamaica, and also spoken to many Jamaicans here in the United States. Many have regretfully told me that much of the knowledge of the ancient practices has been lost. The evils of oppression, economics, and colonization have robbed us all of much helpful information.

Queen Nanny's story is therefore steeped in folklore, and sorting out the truth is a tricky endeavor. She was born in Ghana in either 1865 or 1866, and was killed by British captain William Cuffee during one of the many battles fought to free the enslaved Africans in Jamaica. This powerful foremother's story persists, however, and she has made it into art, literature, and even onto money. In Jamaica she is still honored as a national hero. She is also the only Jamaican woman to have been given the lofty title of "Right Excellent." Nanny reminds us of the strength of our ancestors, and that with them anything is possible.

Queen Nanny Workings

Workings for Queen Nanny can be done when you wish to connect to her warrior spirit, her fierce resolve and resourcefulness, or her undying legacy of resistance. I find her particularly helpful when trying to find fierceness and strength in the face of unjust authorities and when trying to rally the troops for an important cause.

QUEEN NANNY GRIS-GRIS BAG

This special blend is designed to grant the user protection, and deliver them from all forms of oppression and unnecessarily restrictive situations. It is good if you feel particularly stuck in your job, in relationships, at home, or in any other problem areas.

Ingredients

- Small black candle
- 3 tablespoons organic dried hibiscus flowers
- 1 tablespoon dried lime peel
- 1 tablespoon dried horehound
- 1 tablespoon lemongrass
- 1 tablespoon dirt from the crossroads

Gather all the ingredients on your ritual altar. Light the candle. Add the herbs to a small wooden bowl one at a time; then mix with your hands. Add the dirt from the crossroads. Now the mixture is ready for use.

Place a small pinch in each corner of your bedroom; then pour what's remaining into a small natural cloth bag. Carry it with you at all times. When you feel it has done its work (usually after a week or two), bury the bag under the roots of a large tree. ■

MAROON HEALING RITUAL BATH

Much of Obeah is based on the complex use of healing herbs and formulas. Priest Oswan from the Voodoo Spiritual Temple was known as an Obeah man, and his knowledge of herbal magick was vast. Part of his legacy is the useful power of herbs to transform almost any situation. While you should always rely on the benefits of traditional medicine for serious illness, this bath will help to promote healing and divine recovery in all aspects. Prepare and use the bath on the eve of the new moon. Repeat as necessary. You may wish to combine it with candle magick or other workings to increase its benefits.

Ingredients

- 1 gallon spring water
- 1 cup guava nectar
- 1 cup soursop (guanabana) nectar
- 3 tablespoons dried sage
- 1 tablespoon dried elderberries
- 1 tablespoon milk thistle seed

Gather all the ingredients. In a large pot on the stove heat 4 cups of spring water. When it begins to simmer, add the guava and soursop nectars. Secure the sage, elderberries, and milk thistle seed inside a small cloth bag and add this to the water. Simmer for 5 minutes. Remove from heat. Cool and add remaining spring water. Remove the bag with the herbs and seeds. It is now ready to add to your bath. Use one cup of the mixture to a tub full of water. ■

OBEAH OIL

Obeah oil is one of the formulas that is used far and wide. Its power has spread far beyond the local Jamaican community and become a legendary formula. It is used to consecrate sacred spaces and remove negative influences of all kinds. It is best to create this formula on the eve of the full moon.

Ingredients

- 1 ounce sweet almond oil
- 9 drops vetiver oil
- 9 drops myrrh oil
- 9 drops galangal oil
- 9 drops lemon oil
- Small piece of snakeskin

Put all the items in a small glass bottle on your altar. Cap the bottle and then rub it vigorously between your hands. Next throw it gently into the air and catch it to give it the blessings of the spirit world. Now it is ready to use. You can wear it on your person or add it to your ritual bath, candles, and other workings. One thing that I find particularly effective is to add it to a simmering pot while I am creating other formulas or spells. This will help to purify your space, and also isolate it from outside interference. ■

MAROON MAGICK LEMONADE

This lemonade uses traditional Jamaican ingredients to make a drink that is both healing and refreshing.

Ingredients

- 6 cups water
- 1-inch piece of ginger root, peeled
- Peel of 1 whole orange
- Peel of 1 whole lime
- 1 cup honey
- ½ cup hibiscus flowers, dried
- 1 cup lemon juice, freshly squeezed

Boil 2 cups water in a small saucepan over low heat. Add ginger root, orange peel, lime peel, and honey and stir well. Turn heat down to simmer and cook for 1 minute. Remove from heat. Add hibiscus and lemon juice. Cool to room temperature and strain through a cheesecloth into a large pitcher. Add the remaining 4 cups of water. Chill thoroughly and pour over ice. Serves 6. ■

The Ashe of Marie Laveau and the Voodoo queens lives on today. They showed us how to have compassion, resourcefulness, and tenacity in the face of all obstacles. They took what little they had on hand and created empires. These queens are truly an inspirational force helping us continue to fight the good fight today.

12

POMBA GIRA AND SANTA MUERTE: DEATH AND THE CROSSROADS

So much of African traditional religion is based on the sacred energy of time and space. You will hear devotees in La Regla Lucumi, and other manifestations of the religions, refer to being on their "proper path." This is probably one of the reasons that deities governing the crossroads like Pomba Gira, Exú, and others are so important. There are several other orishas, goddesses, loas, and queens that you may wish to connect with that are certainly worthy of note. I wish I could give them each a chapter of their own, but then this would be a multivolume work. I would be remiss, however, if I failed to include two of the most popular women in this realm, especially in modern times. They have shown us their glory and power for ages, and I respectfully hope to present some of their majesty here.

Pomba Gira

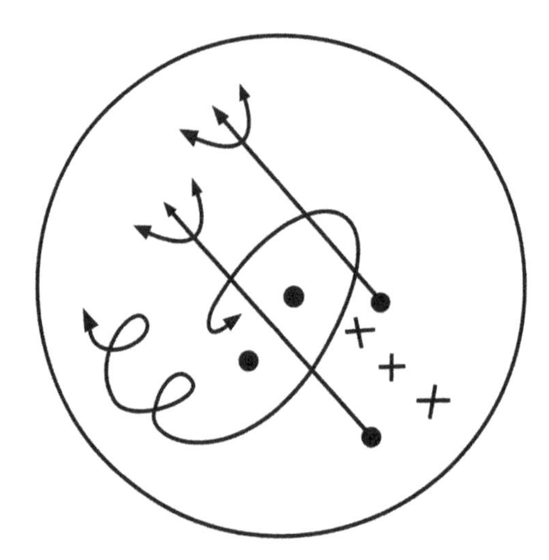

Pomba Gira, with her unabashed sexuality, power, and control, is a feminine force who is honored by many. She is an orixa (Brazilian orisha) honored in Umbanda and Candomble. Like many of the other African traditional religions, Umbanda and Candomble often incorporate both indigenous and more traditionally European practices in their magick. I believe this is largely due to necessity. As with the other religions, knowledge was handed down orally, and very often was shrouded in secrecy.

Described as the wife of Exu, Pomba Gira, the wild woman who spins the world, is shrouded in much mystery and darkness. She is outwardly brazen, very often depicted with bare breasts, and sporting a full necklace of skulls, giving new meaning to the word *bling*. Pomba Gira embodies all that is free and unashamed about sexual pleasure in yourself and the wider world. Many times, when she manifests in ritual, she is known to tell secrets and reveal confidences, urging people to own their actions and also to take pride in them. Pomba Gira holds much mystery in the folds of her skirts, where she is said to shelter all who seek relief from the pain of a broken heart. She is said not to come in judgment, but in a deep and abiding understanding because she has been there, seen all, and done everything.

There are many different avatars, or manifestations, of Pomba Gira, and each one occupies a unique place and function. Included in this group are Pomba Gira Mundo, the world spinner who keeps the whole world turning on its axis. There is a Pomba Gira Sete Encruzadas, the embodiment of the Ashe of the seven crossroads. Pomba Gira das Almas is the Pomba Gira of the souls. There is a Pomba Gira das Cobras, said to command serpents. The seashore has its own manifestation called Pomba Gira Maria da Praia.

At least one of the manifestations of this orixa is based on an actual person, this is the case with Pomba Gira Maria Padilha. She is given the utmost respect at all times, and is seen as a force of extremes. Her domain is most often love and sexual unions. She is particularly featured in the spirituality of sex workers. I know one group of strippers who set up a shrine to her backstage, and she granted them great wealth and success for every dollar they stuffed into her spiritual G-string. She understands the importance of money, and more importantly what individuals sometimes have to do to survive and thrive.

Pomba Gira Sete Saias ("seven skirts") is described as a fierce and powerful force working with a quickness. Like many of the other Pomba Giras, she helps with romance and pain in the heart. She is honored with both dance and drums.

Legend tells us that many of these different energies had their roots in Portugal, like many Brazilian people. Each separate spiritual house has its own slightly different origin story, each unique and valid. There are several other manifestations of her too. A partial list follows:

- Pomba Gira da Calunga: Pomba Gira Who Sings
- Pomba Gira das Almas: Pomba Gira of the Souls
- Pomba Gira das Cobras: Pomba Gira of the Snakes
- Pomba Gira da Estrela: Pomba Gira of the Stars
- Pomba Gira da Lua: Pomba Gira of the Moon

- Pomba Gira Dama da Noite: Pomba Gira, Lady of the Night
- Pomba Gira dos Infernos: Pomba Gira of the Two Infernos
- Pomba Gira Cigana de Fé: Pomba Gira Gypsy of Faith
- Pomba Gira Rosa Caveira: Pomba Gira of the Rose Skull
- Pomba Gira Maria Molambo: Pomba Gira of the Trash
- Pomba Gira Maria Navala: Pomba Gira of the Razor Blade

Red and black are the traditional colors used in honoring Pomba Gira. You can see this represented in statues for her and other artwork. Because she is seen as the wife of Exú, her ritual day is Monday, the same as his. Some houses do assign Friday to her as well.

Unlike many of the other orixas and loas, she is said to demand payment and offerings both before and after undertaking any workings. Patrons will leave a small offering when the request is made, and then a much larger one when their wishes are granted. She is very frequently petitioned for the return of a wayward lover. Although the logic and ethics of this will be questioned by some, nonetheless this is part of her function. My best advice in these situations is to truly be careful what you wish for, as I have seen it backfire in more cases than not.

Herbs and Offerings for the Pomba Giras

It is most common to leave offerings for the Pomba Giras at the crossroads, or the corner outside of a busy bar or nightclub.

- Abre camino
- Aniseed
- Basil
- Carnations
- Cigarillos
- Dark rum
- Gin
- Honey
- Manioc flour
- Peony
- Red roses
- Red wine
- Sage
- Tobacco

SHRINE FOR POMBA GIRA

Unlike some of the other altars and shrines we have talked about, Pomba Gira's ritual items are, in keeping with tradition, set on the floor, or directly on the pavement. Please take extra caution if you choose to set yours up this way, as placing candles on the floor means they must be given even extra attention so as not to walk or bump into them. As I have mentioned, there are many different Pomba Giras, so please be mindful and selective about the items you are using and do your best to choose things that are appropriate.

Ingredients

- Rose water
- Red and/or black cloth
- Statue or image of Pomba Gira
- Red and/or black candle
- 3 drops sage oil
- 3 drops patchouli oil
- Red carnations
- 3 peony seeds
- Glass of dry red wine
- Other offerings for Pomba Gira

Gather all the ingredients where you are going to set up the altar or shrine. Wash down the area thoroughly with rose water and spread out your cloth. On the left, place the image of Pomba Gira. On the right side, place the candle. Light the candle. After it has been burning for a few minutes and the wax has begun to liquefy, carefully add the oils. Next place the flowers, red wine, and other offerings in the space. If you like, you may say a prayer or other words of ritual praise for Pomba Gira, such as "Saravá Pomba Gira." Your space is now ready for worship and magick. ■

POMBA GIRA CANDLE

This ritual candle for Pomba Gira will help you when you are at a crossroads; she is known for opening doors and removing all barriers. But just like her husband Exú, solutions can be tricky yet highly effective.

Ingredients

- 7-day removable candle in glass (red or with an image of Pomba Gira)
- 3 drops cinnamon oil
- Pinch of lodestone

Assemble all the ingredients on your ritual space or shrine. With a toothpick or porcupine quill, draw an equal-armed cross or crossroads on the top of your candle. Add the cinnamon oil; then sprinkle with the lodestone.

Say the following prayer for Pomba Gira:

Move the Air!
Transform the Fire!
Water Becomes!
Earth Heals!
Hail Pomba Gira!
Hear My Prayer!

Then you may light the candle. Burn it each day until it is finished, remembering never to leave a burning candle unattended. If you must, snuff it out and light it again as soon as possible. ■

POMBA GIRA OIL

Wear this oil whenever you want to feel the sensual strength and power of Pomba Gira. She is known to triumph over all her enemies, no matter how large or small.

Ingredients

- ½ ounce sweet almond oil
- 7 drops carnation oil
- 7 drops rose oil
- 7 anise seeds, crushed

Assemble all ingredients on your ritual altar or sacred space. Add the oils and seeds to a small glass bottle. Rub the bottle between your hands. Then raise the bottle up, down, and side to side, making the symbol of a crossroads. Then it is charged and ready for use. ■

POMBA GIRA BLESSING WATER

In Candomble and Umbanda, blessing water is frequently used to remove obstacles and guide you toward your true destiny. This formula is best prepared on a Monday during the waxing moon. This formula includes Abre Camino oil, which can be found online or at your local botanica.

Ingredients

- 3 cups spring water
- 21 drops Abre Camino oil
- 3 drops sage oil

Gather all ingredients in your sacred space. Place a glass jar in the center of your altar or shrine. Add the spring water and the oils. Stir clockwise with a wooden spoon. Now your mixture is ready for use.

One of the beautiful things about this water is that you can use it as often as you like. It can be sprinkled on the threshold before leaving the house, or at the crossroads. After sprinkling out the water, step over it and do not turn back. ■

HOMEMADE ANISETTE FOR POMBA GIRA

Anisette is one of Pomba Gira's most treasured offerings. With this recipe you can easily make your own. It may take some time, but the wait is worth it.

Ingredients

- 1 cup star anise
- 1 tablespoon fennel seeds
- 1 liter vodka
- ¾ cup sugar

Gather all ingredients together. Heat a frying pan over medium heat and add the anise and fennel seeds. Toast for about 1 minute—you should begin to smell them. Remove the seeds from the heat and set aside to cool. Crush the seeds using a mortar and pestle and pour the mixture into a cloth bag.

Pour the vodka into a glass jar and add the seed bag. Cover and shake well. Leave the jar in a dark place for 4 or 5 days. Remove the seed bag and discard. Strain the vodka through a cheesecloth.

Heat sugar and ¾ cup water in a small saucepan over medium heat. Bring to a boil, stirring frequently, until the sugar is dissolved. Remove from heat and add to the vodka. Cool completely. This is now ready for use.

You may leave an offering of anisette on your altar or shrine, or pour some out at the crossroads. Keep refrigerated and use within 6 months. This concoction is strong, so please use caution and drink responsibly. ■

HERBAL GRIS-GRIS FOR POMBA GIRA DAMA DA NOITE

This Pomba Gira is honored when help is needed with work-related issues. Devotees also call on her when they are having trouble with child support payments and related matters. Pomba Gira Dama da Noite is known for being sweet and gentle. She is especially partial to night-blooming jasmine, so use that type of oil to anoint your mixture if possible.

Ingredients

- 3 tablespoons dried red rose petals, crushed
- 1 tablespoon ground sage
- 1 tablespoon tobacco
- 3 drops jasmine oil

Combine all ingredients on your ritual table or altar. Place the rose petals, sage, and tobacco in a large wooden bowl (preferably bamboo). Sprinkle the jasmine oil over. Mix well. Carry the mixture in a small cloth bag in your pocket, or close to your heart, until solutions to your problems begin to appear. You may then dispose of the herbs at a crossroads. Remember to not look back. ■

Santa Muerte

The lovely face of death worship, La Santa Muerte's popularity has grown exponentially in recent years. Also known as Mother of Impossibility, the Bony Lady, Patron of a Good Death, Grim Reapress, White Sister, or Santisima Muerte, she is a powerful force to be reckoned with. By some estimates, there are over twelve million devotees of Santa Muerte worldwide. At her core, Santa Muerte is cosmically Mexican. Some may question her inclusion here; however, the complicated story of her origins varies depending on whom you are asking. Some believe she may be connected to African-derived practices, and it is certainly true that she has taken up residence in many La Regla Lucumi botanicas and religious stores. Even if her roots are disputed, her modern manifestations, rites, and rituals have a prominent place in the lives of many Afro-Latinx practitioners.

She is known as a folk saint, meaning she operates outside the boundaries of the Catholic Church. Actually, she has been repeatedly denounced by the Church as an evil and satanic influence. The FBI doesn't like her either, saying she is an icon of criminals involved in the narcotics trade. True, she does indeed have a reputation as being a popular saint to pray to for those who are involved in dangerous pursuits. Worship of Santa Muerte has also spread widely among the incarcerated in the United States and throughout the world. But prisoners aren't the only ones honoring Santa Muerte; she is still honored by many different groups. In her role as champion of the oppressed and marginalized, this fierce goddess has taken up residence in the hearts and minds of many in the LGBTQ community, particularly outside of Mexico.

In many ways this Bony Lady has even become a marketing and media star lately. As with the other goddesses and orishas, you can buy statuary of her, but there are also T-shirts, tattoos, and several movies and television shows that highlight her presence. She has made an appearance in *Breaking Bad* and *American Horror Story*, and will even be featured in the next installment of the *Bad Boys* film franchise. It seems the appeal of this captivating feminine force knows almost no bounds, just like death itself.

The Dark Faces of Death

There are many orishas, loas, and goddesses of death that appear in this book. Both Oya and Maman Brigitte grace these pages. However, I felt that this work would not be complete without adding Santa Muerte. Even though she isn't an orisha or loa, she features prominently in the religious life of many ATR practitioners. As it has been observed, Death does indeed have many dark faces. Consequently, representations of Santa Muerte have many faces as well. There are statues that simply look like the classic grim reaper, and those in white, black, red, gold, blue, green, and purple. Each colored cloak is said to have its own function and represents the corresponding path of Santa Muerte. There are statues that are poised to see no evil, hear no evil, and speak no evil—and even ones dressed in tutus. I have seen some very early representations of Santa Muerte that mimic a Cupid figure, and more modern ones that are almost the same as the Mexican Day of the Dead figure known as Lolita.

Offerings for Santa Muerte

Offerings for Santa Muerte are viewed in every possible way as gifts that are shared between friends. This is particularly true when she is offered cigarettes (made from tobacco or marijuana). Devotees traditionally offer cigarettes to her in a particular way: either they offer two, smoking one themselves and leaving the other for her in an ashtray; or they smoke one and blow the smoke into the face of her statue. This blowing smoke onto a statue is common in African traditional religions. A word also needs to be said about offering flowers to Santa Muerte. Some practitioners only give fresh flowers, while others give those that have started to wilt and are on their way to dying. If you are new to working with Santa Muerte, I would consider doing divination beforehand to figure out which type of flower she needs from you. Here's a list of common offerings for Santa Muerte:

- Avocados
- Beer
- Brandy
- Chocolate
- Cigarettes
- Copal
- Dittany of Crete (rare)
- Gardenias
- Marigolds
- Marijuana
- Peaches
- Peppermint
- Plums
- Pomegranates
- Rosemary
- Rue
- Rum
- Sandalwood
- Sherry
- Tequila
- Tobacco
- Tulips
- White bread

SETTING A SHRINE FOR SANTA MUERTE

It is customary for shrines to Santa Muerte to be set up facing west.

Items

- Altar cloth
- Candle for Santa Muerte
- Image of Santa Muerte
- Glass of water
- Glass of rum, tequila, or other liquor
- 2 cigarettes
- Other offerings for Santa Muerte

Lay your cloth out on the space. Place the candle and the image for Santa Muerte in the center of the cloth. Place the glass of water to the right of the candle, and the glass of liquor to the left. Light the candle, and as it is burning explain to Santa Muerte the issues you are dealing with. Then light one of the cigarettes and place it in an ashtray in front of the image. Smoke the other cigarette yourself, if you smoke. (If you don't smoke, take the cigarette to a crossroads near your home and leave it there. Turn around and don't look back.) Then leave the rest of the offerings on the cloth for Santa Muerte. ■

SANTA MUERTE CANDLE WORKING

Very often Santa Muerte is offered candles as a way to honor her and get her help with troubling situations. As I have noted, each different-colored representation is used for a different purpose. Red signifies love and passion, white is most often healing, black represents protection from enemies, gold or yellow is for money and financial abundance, green is for justice and legal issues, and purple is for spiritual development and psychic connection. At my botanica in Brooklyn, we have more Santa Muerte candles than any other kind. (Maybe this says something about my neighborhood.) Anyway, this working will allow you to get help on several different fronts, and for that reason a seven-colored Santa Muerte candle is called for. These candles can be used for help with love, protection, justice, and more. Simply add your specific desires to the petition.

Ingredients

- 7-day 7-color candle for Santa Muerte
- 3 drops copal oil
- 3 drops sandalwood oil
- 3 drops peppermint oil

Place the candle on your working altar or shrine. Poke three holes into the top with a toothpick or pin and add the oils. Rub the candle between your hands to awaken it and charge it with your own energy. As you light the candle, humbly say the following Santa Muerte prayer:

> Holy Death, I beg of and salute your immortal power.
> Hear my pleas and look favorably on my wishes.
> (State your wishes.)
> I thank you for all that you are, all that you have done, and
> all that you will continue to do for me.

This candle should be allowed to burn down until it is completely finished. If you need to extinguish it and relight it later, say the prayer each time you light the candle. You may also wish to strengthen your working by leaving offerings of cigarettes, liquor, and/or flowers. ■

PAN DE MUERTO (BREAD FOR THE DEAD)

In Mexico this bread is made on October 31, November 1, and November 2 as an offering to the ancestors and to ask for their protection and guidance for the coming year. It is also a customary offering for the Bony Lady. This recipe may seem complicated, but don't worry—as you go through the steps, all will be revealed about how to make this delicious treat for Santa Muerte.

Ingredients

- ¼ cup vegetable shortening
- ¼ cup milk
- ¼ cup warm water
- 2 cups all-purpose flour
- 1 cup bread flour
- 1 ¼ teaspoons active dry yeast
- ½ teaspoon sea salt

- ¼ cup sugar
- 2 eggs, beaten
- 3 teaspoons orange zest
- 1 teaspoon lemon zest
- 3 tablespoons sugar
- ¼ cup freshly squeezed orange juice
- 2 tablespoons orange blossom water
- 2 tablespoons sugar

Melt the shortening in a saucepan over low heat; then add the milk and bring to a simmer. Remove from heat; then add the warm water.

In a separate bowl, combine 1 cup all-purpose flour and 1 cup bread flour. Mix with the yeast, sea salt, and sugar.

Gradually add the milk mixture to the flour mixture, stirring well after each addition. Then add the eggs and 2 teaspoons of orange zest. Finally, add the remaining cup of all-purpose flour.

Knead the dough on a floured surface for 5 minutes or until it is smooth. Next, place the dough into a bowl, cover it with a cloth, and leave it to rise in a warm and draft-free location for at least an hour, or until it has doubled in size.

Place the dough on a floured surface again. Punch down and knead. Then you are ready to shape the loaf. Traditionally, in Mexico the bread is shaped into a circle with either a cross or smaller circles or balls on the top. Feel free to be ambitious and shape your loaf how you want it. I have even seen people incorporate skulls into the bread's design.

After you have your desired shape, cover and let it rise again until doubled in size. While this is happening, preheat your oven to 350 degrees. When the loaf is fully risen, bake for 30 to 40 minutes or until the bread is golden brown. Remove from oven.

The next step is to prepare the glaze for the top of the loaf. In a small saucepan over low heat, warm the remaining orange and lemon zest, orange juice, orange blossom water, and 3 tablespoons sugar. Remove from heat when the sugar has melted. While the loaf is slightly warm, brush the top of it with the glaze. Then sprinkle with the last 2 tablespoons of sugar. Now it is ready to serve to Santa Muerte, or whomever else you wish. ■

SANTA MUERTE INFUSED TEQUILA

A popular way to connect with Santa Muerte is to offer her a drink. The following recipe soaks flowers and spices in tequila to create a truly delicious creation fit for the divine. During the Day of the Dead festivities in Mexico, marigolds are used to honor those who have gone before and guide the dead to their altars. You can drink this yourself to help find the guidance and messages you need to hear from Santa Muerte and the ancestors.

Ingredients

- 2 cups tequila
- ½ cup edible organic marigold blossoms
- 1 stick cinnamon
- 1 sprig rosemary
- Image of Santa Muerte

Gather all your ingredients together. Pour tequila into a large glass jar. Add the marigolds, cinnamon, and rosemary. Screw the lid on the jar and shake well. Place on top of the image of Santa Muerte and leave in a cool, dark place for seven days. It should develop a deep golden color.

Strain the tequila through a cheesecloth, and share the first drink with Santa Muerte. Now you may bottle the mixture. Keep refrigerated and use within 2 weeks. ■

In my estimation, the popularity of Santa Muerte will continue to rise. Death is the final freedom and the ultimate equalizer. People who struggle with getting freedom, justice, and equality will continue to turn to her as their only hope. Perhaps because of, or in spite of, her condemnation and exclusion from mainstream religious practices, she has moved into all remaining available spaces. Her quasi-saint status means she can be asked for assistance and favors in much the same way as traditional saints. As in the candle spell above, we also can see how some of the practices and methods from La Regla Lucumi can be put into use. Santa Muerte also uses traditional herbs like copal and maguey from Curanderismo, or Mexican shamanic healing. Who knows where she will go next?

Marienette

There is one other loa that I feel needs a place here in this discussion about the dark feminine. Her name is Marienette. Marienette is a Petro loa who is known for her fierceness and destructive powers. She is the consort of Ti Jean, a Petro loa who resides in the dense bushes. She has as her animal companions both owls and loup-garou (the legendary Haitian werewolf).

In artwork she is represented by the Catholic image of Anima Sola. This image depicts a chained woman suffering in the flames of purgatory. In all her manifestations she is said to be full of great rage. I do not recommend setting up an altar or table for her unless advised to do so by your spiritual elders.

The power of the sacred feminine takes many forms. It can grace the shores of Cuba and the jungles of Brazil. Each goddess, orisha, and loa holds a unique energy and message for us. Pomba Gira can help us with acceptance and sexual freedom. Santa Muerte inhabits the mysterious spaces of death.

CONCLUSION

In many ways, these orishas, loas, goddesses, and queens truly defy explanation. As Priestess Miriam of the Voodoo Spiritual Temple in New Orleans likes to remind me: "Once you label these things, try to define them, you force them into a shape, a vessel which makes it limited." The concepts presented in African traditional religions are limitless, and the abilities of its followers are limitless too. We can learn the stories, the offerings, the dances, the rhythms, the songs, but we must also actively seek the guidance of our elders and teachers in order to be able to discover our true path. It has always been done this way. This path is different for each person, and your guides will help you get where you need to go.

Within these pages you have hopefully found orishas, loas, goddesses, and Voodoo queens that empower, inspire, and elevate you. You may even have found some that shock or scare you. Remember that they represent the full range of sacred feminine possibility and existence. These strengths have sustained them throughout the ages, and hopefully you will find ways to help them strengthen you too. Maybe you will start with a ritual shrine or altar, or maybe by simply making a meal to share with your daughters, your mother, and your loved ones. Hopefully, if you wish to continue on your journey in one of the African traditional religions, you will find helpful babalawos (Ifa priests), santeros or santeras (Lucumi priests or priestesses), houngans or mambos (Haitian priests or priestesses), or other teachers to guide you on your proper path for your highest good. You will find a spiritually nurturing community that will help you just as these feminine forces do on a cosmic level.

This book begins with the orishas Oshún and Yemaya who show us the absolute power and beauty of water in the river and in the ocean. Their strength is in their kindness, their gentleness, their sensuality, their nurturing wisdom. In contrast, we have the orisha Oya, a warrior in every way who shoots lightning bolts at her obstacles. She is the walking embodiment of change. Nana Buruku is an orisha who brings the healing and wisdom of the ancients everywhere she goes. This book would not have been complete without Mami Wata. Not just a single entity, Mami Wata is the spirit of all the waters in the world. She helps us to feel this sacred element on every level.

Next, we turn our sacred attention to the loa from the Haitian Vodou and New Orleans Voodoo pantheon. These are not thought of as traditional goddesses but instead sacred feminine forces in the universe that guide us. We start with the Erzulies, the beating hearts of our desires and experiences with love. Much of modern spirituality has become reductionist, but each Erzulie loa is separate and should always be viewed as such. Realizing this will assist you in all realms of love magick. It has always been true that one of the most important elements of magick is believing; this is only one of the joyous lessons that the loa Aida Wedo shares with us. The glorious serpent of the rainbow shows us that light and beauty can be right around the bend during even the darkest storms. The loa La Sirene can sing a song of illusion or one of hidden secrets and guide us divinely toward our own truths. The powerful loa Ayizan is simultaneously the first Voodoo priestess and every mambo who has reigned since. She shows us the benefits and the beauty of initiation on every possible level. She is the Ashe, or life force, behind these divine transformations, peeking her mysteries out from behind a blessed curtain of waving palm fronds. New Orleans Voodoo is like no other religion. It is informed by the unique and delicious character of the magickal city. Turning assumptions and expectations on their head as if they were tossed in the Mississippi River, the loa and practices that manifest here are delightful and diverse. We see certain loa triumph here like nowhere else, and two of these are Annie Christmas and Maman Brigitte. Annie Christmas represents an archetype that may be familiar to many of us, the strong, muscular, gender-fluid female that excels in nontraditional ways. She reminds us that this power is available to all when needed. Maman Brigitte holds a special place in my heart. I have always felt like the cemetery was comfortable, like a second home. The powerful dead contained within their gates are governed by Maman Brigitte, who dances among them with lacy skirts and maybe even roses in her hair. She shows us that death is not the ultimate end, but a beginning of a different kind of existence. She can bring justice and help to balance the problems in our lives.

Any discussion about spirituality in New Orleans needs to talk about the legendary Voodoo queen Marie Laveau. Powerful, resourceful, and still honored throughout the city today, she is in many ways the face of the religion. Everyone in the city feels a connection to her, and she hears all their prayers. For over a hundred years she has fueled the power of the psychic practices, and in this book you find many ways to honor and connect with her divine presence. There have also been many more queens of New Orleans Voodoo, including Priestess Miriam Chamani, whom I dearly love and respect. Then there are other queens that we may choose to honor on our spiritual journey, including Queen Nanny of Jamaica, who led so many on their journey to freedom. Queen Nzinga from present-day Angola was a visionary and a strong foremother to modern warrior women everywhere.

Our final chapter includes more orishas and saints from further afield, powerful feminine forces who have vitally important lessons for those who wish to listen. There is Pomba Gira from Brazil, who revels in her sexual power and ability. And Santa Muerte from Mexico who has been called to help in almost every situation. And while she may not be an orisha, loa, or goddess, she functions in the same ways to bless and assist all who honor her. She literally comes in all colors to help her followers navigate all different realms.

In some instances, you will be called by these feminine forces to choose; in others, you will be gracefully chosen. Hopefully, what you have found here are the tried-and-true methods, never for commanding the orishas, loas, goddesses, and Voodoo queens, but instead for understanding them better, connecting with and respectfully recognizing them and yourself in the physical and spiritual worlds. I believe this is possible for everyone. Like all good things, this book is meant to be a bountiful beginning on a path that will become aided by your teachers and elders as more is revealed on your journey. Ashe!

ACKNOWLEDGMENTS

Many thanks and much love always to Priestess Miriam Chamani, Gros Mambo Bonnie Devlin, Ochun Olukari Al'aye, Ogbe Di, Nia Dorsey, Aria Dorsey, Grace Buterbaugh, Alice Licato, Prudy Dorsey, Edith Licato, Christian, Siona, Michele, Vincent, Victoria, Tish, Tavia, Mel, Dot, Glenn, Mark, Amanda, Christina, Windafire, Indigo Ortiz, Emi, Lennora Spicer, Rebeca Spirit, Bruce Baker, Sam and Ezra Visnic, Liam Nadeau, Phoenyx Precil, Scarlett Precil, Riva Nyri Precil, Mina Bellavia, Cayne Miceli, Little Luna, Phat ManDee, Cleomili Harris, Julio Jean, Sabine Blaizin, Jason Mankey, Lisi Tribble, Joy Wedmedyk, Clarivel Ruiz, Sen Elias, Risa Sharpe, Faye Ginsburg, Addison Smith, Louis Martinie, Mishlen Linden, Heather Killen, Arthur Lipp-Bonewits, Mychael Scribner, Jason Winslade, Spenser Adams, Tom Schneider, Vychtor Kossler, Freakee Dalton, Berta Daniels, Starr Ann Ravenhawk, Chris Cary, Kevin Pelrine, Devin Hunter, Devin Person, John Driver, Margot Adler, Frances Denny, Cristina Esteras-Ortiz, Phoenix Williams, Cat Thagard, David Lewis-Laurent, Peter Turner, Heather Greene, Bruce "Sunpie" Barnes, Witchdoctor Utu and the Dragon Ritual Drummers, and all my honored ancestors.

A special heartfelt thanks also goes out to my own goddesses, orishas, and loas who walk with and protect me. There is Lilith, queen of the night, who claimed this existence before I was even born. The argument can be made that Lilith is a goddess for our time, or for all time, really. Many modern witches and feminists have taken up her tribute and see her as a powerful force for gender equality and protection. Lilith reminds us what is truly and primally feminine in all forms. Here I am making a firm distinction between primal and primitive. These are the ancient sacred places where darkness lets in light, and where coal is transformed into diamond, through constant and sustained pressure and power.

Then there is Hel, patron of my maternal ancestors the Holburns. Hel (aka Hela, or Hella) is a Norse goddess named for the World of the Dead, where she lives. Some conceptualize her as a giant, while others cast her as queen of the underworld. Hel reminds us that sometimes we have to face reality and mortality. Hers is a stark realism. One of her traits is helping the less fortunate, the sick, and the poor. She has seen me through all these times.

Oshún, who I am told owns my head. I find you in the depths of life's sweetness and also its tears. I will keep coming to the river and basking in the love and majesty I find there.

Maman Brigitte, my mother, who helps me find truth and justice on even the darkest nights. Your silence means there are no words but only the most powerful love.

I never would have made it without you.

Appendix A

HERBS FOR THE ORISHAS, LOAS, AND GODDESSES

The following herbs and botanicals can be given as offerings or used to create your own magickal spells to bring about necessary change.

Acacia (*Acacia spp.*): Ruled by the element of air and the sun, this is used for meditation and protection, and to increase psychic power. It is a sacred offering for Osiris and Ra. It is a common ingredient in spells.

Allspice (*Pimenta dioica, Pimenta officinalis*): This spice is derived from the berry of an evergreen tree and is connected to the element of fire and the planet Mars. It is a favorite of the orishas Yemaya and Oshún, and the goddesses Venus and Aphrodite. Add it to your magickal workings for love, success, fertility, healing, and compassion.

Almond (*Prunus dulcis*): Both the nut and oil are considered sacred to the goddess Hecate. People often use sweet almond as a base oil, which many of the formulas in this book call for. Almond is good for spellwork dealing with abundance, wealth, luck, clarity, and wisdom.

It is also useful for removing negative energy and banishing. Mercury is the planet governing this plant, as well as the element of air.

Angelica (*Angelica archangelica*): Sacred to the goddess Brigid, the root of this plant is used in both Celtic and Hoodoo magick. It is also called masterwort, archangel root, or my favorite, holy ghost root. Angelica root is used for protection, healing, warding off sickness and evil, and luck and gambling magick. Elementally, it is associated with fire and ruled by the planet Venus.

Aniseed (*Pimpinella anisum*): Used as an offering for the orisha Oya and the orixa Pomba Gira, this tiny seed is said to bring protection, purification, and harmony. It is connected to the planet Jupiter and the element of air.

Apple (*Malis pumila*): This common fruit is used in magick for love, divination, and healing. Remember the old saying, "An apple a day keeps the doctor away"? Well, apples can protect you from all sorts of things, not just illness. Because of the biblical myth, they are considered sacred to the goddess Lilith. Apples are also a traditional offering for the goddesses Hel and Hecate and the folk saint Santa Muerte. They are ruled by the element of water, and the planet Venus or Jupiter.

Basil (*Ocimum basilicum*): Basil has been used for centuries as a holy herb. It is found in the practices of the Ancient Romans and also Eastern cultures. It is sacred to both the orixa Pomba Gira and the goddess Brigid. Basil is ruled by Mars and falls under the element of fire.

Bay Leaf (*Laurus nobilis*): The two main uses for this kitchen herb are protection and love. It is ruled by the element of fire and is said to also aid with psychic vision and insight. It is offered to the goddess Hecate. Bay leaf is seen as an herb of the sun.

Bergamot (*Citrus bergamia*): This is used for success, money, and divine joy. It can be added to almost any working. A member of the mint family, bergamot is governed by the element of fire and the sun.

Blackberry (*Rubus fruticosus*): These plants are very similar to roses, containing thorns, white flowers, and dark purple berries. Celtic myth tells us that they were associated with both the Devil and Christ and used to keep away vampires. They are sacred to the goddess Brigid. Aries and fire are said to rule the thorns, while the leaves are governed by Scorpio and Venus. In Hoodoo traditions, the thorns are used in magick for setting hard boundaries. Blackberry is also useful in magick for healing, protection, and wealth.

Camphor (*Cinnamomum camphora*): Its uses all revolve around protection from negative energy, sickness, and other creepy things. However, it is also an effective ingredient when used as a component in spellwork for luck, divination, psychic ability, prosperity, and love. It is considered sacred to the goddess Lilith, and the orisha Oya and also Yemaya. Elementally it is associated with water, and it can be used in workings connecting to the moon. It frequently comes in small white squares that will evaporate over time.

Cardamom (*Elettaria cardamomum*): Offered to the goddess Lilith and also the loa Erzulie Freda Dahomey, this herb is said to bring joy, energy, and romance to the situation at hand. It is ruled by the planet Venus and the element of water, and is also considered a powerful aphrodisiac.

Carnation (*Dianthus caryophyllus*): These bring blessings of healing and love. They are especially good for healing from past trauma. White carnations can be given to the orisha Yemaya, while purple and red ones are given to the orisha Oya. Carnations are ruled by the sun and the element of fire.

Chamomile (*Matricaria chamomilla*): Sacred to Brigid and a host of other goddesses, this common herb is said to promote sleep and prophetic dreams. When you grow them, many varieties will form a carpet creeping gently across the garden. The tiny yellow and white flowers are also said to help with luck, protection, and gentle love. I find this especially useful when working with children. It is associated with the moon and the element of water.

Cinnamon (*Cinnamomum zeylanicum*): Ruled by the sun, this botanical is sacred to the goddesses, loas, and orishas. Lilith, Oshún, Erzulie Freda Dahomey, Pomba Gira, and others are offered this spice. It is primarily used in love and sex magick, and for healing. Cinnamon is connected to Mars and the sun and can be used in workings that call on these energies.

Clover (*Trifolium spp.*): Ruled by air, these small flowers are sacred to the goddess Brigid. Just like the four-leaf clovers of lore, they are known for luck and success, as well as money, protection, and love. Red clovers are associated with the planet Mars.

Cloves (*Eugenia caryophyllata*): Sacred to the goddesses Lilith and Hel and the orisha Oshún, this spice brings passion and abundance. When carried, they are said to have the ability to stop people from gossiping and speaking badly about you. Astrologically, they are governed by Saturn and associated with the element of fire.

Coffee (*Rubiaceae spp.*): Coffee is used as an offering for Pomba Gira and the Norse goddess Hel. Just like with tea, coffee is a tool that can be used for divination. Not surprisingly, it is also used to magically bring energy, focus, and concentration. It has many planetary connections, including Mercury, Jupiter, and Neptune, and is thought to be connected to the element of earth.

Copal (*Protium copal*): This is one of the oldest known holy resins. It was used in Ancient Egypt and also has its place in Central America. Ruled by the sun, it can be burned as a sacred offering to the goddess Lilith and also Santa Muerte.

Cotton (*Gossypium spp.*): Sacred to Maman Brigitte, one technique is to cover her offerings in cotton to be sure they are well received. The plant is native to the Americas, Africa, and India. Many times in this book I have recommended using a natural fiber cloth in your magick; cotton is one of the best materials for this use. It is used for healing, luck, and protection, and it is said even to have the ability to bring rain. It looks like small clouds and as such is associated with the element of air.

Cypress (*Cupressus*): Used to honor the goddesses Hecate, Hera, Athena, Aphrodite, and Astarte, and the orishas Oya and Nana Buruku, this wood is often featured in ritual tools and even Beltane Maypoles. It represents renewal, healing, trust, balance, protection, and prosperity, and is known to help with difficult legal matters and grieving. Cypress is ruled by the earth, the planet Saturn, and the sign of Pisces.

Daisy (*Chrysanthemum leucanthemum*): Ruled by the planet Venus, this is useful for many things beyond just amorous encounters. People use daisies for baby blessings, healing, joy, and divination workings. Some say it is connected to the element of water, while others find it very grounding. There are many different types of daisy: shasta, gerbera, and the rest. They all carry similar properties in their magick. Some Christians associate the daisy with the Virgin Mary, and therefore divine peace and purity. Some Norse practitioners consider them sacred to the goddess Freya, and find them helpful during childbirth.

Dandelion (*Taraxacum officinale*): This little herb goes by several different names: priest's-crown, Irish daisy, blowball, piss-a-bed, white endive, and lion's-tooth. It is associated with the zodiac sign of Leo and the element of air. Dandelions are sacred to the goddesses Brigid and Hecate. It is especially useful in divination magick. Consider placing some dried dandelion flowers next to your tarot cards or runes.

Dill (*Anethum graveolens*): Dill can be used for communication, protection, and luck. It is used as an offering to the goddesses Brigid and Freya and the orisha Oya. Mercury is the ruling planet for this plant, which is associated with the elements of fire and earth.

Dittany of Crete (*Origanum dictamnus*): Also called Cretan Dittany or hop marjoram, this herb dates back to Minoan times in the twenty-seventh century B.C.E. It is sacred to the goddess Hecate and the Mexican Santa Muerte. Medically it has antifungal and anti-inflammatory properties, and it is said to grant love and prophecy.

It is also useful in dream workings and with astral travel. It is associated with the moon and the element of fire. Note: It can be very difficult to obtain the actual herb commercially. There are no universally accepted substitutes, so if it is unobtainable, consider doing a different spell or offering.

Elm (*Ulmus spp.*): This strong, majestic tree is connected with Scorpio and the element of earth. It is sacred to the goddess Lilith. It is used for defense, protection, compassion, communication, and love. The tree is ruled by the planet Earth and the elements of earth and air. Elm is a great wood to use when crafting magickal tools.

Eucalyptus (*Eucalyptus globulus*): Also known as Tasmanian blue gum, this is an extraordinary healing plant. It is a fragrant herbal that is ruled by the moon and the element of water. It is used as an offering for the orisha Yemaya. In addition to healing, eucalyptus is known to promote concentration, restore balance, and enhance divination acts and psychic ability. You can also use it in spells to assist with anxiety and panic.

Fennel (*Foeniculum vulgare*): Both the seeds and the bulbous root of this plant are used in magick and cooking. Sacred to Lilith, this is used for psychic ability, healing, courage, strength, energy, protection, fertility, and love. It is ruled by the planet Mercury and the element of air.

Frankincense (*Boswellia carterii*): Frankincense has many uses. It is said to bring one peace and protection, release unnecessary stress, remove anxiety, and connect one with the divine. Some believe it helps to connect the root chakra with the solar plexis and moves the energy up through to the higher realms. It is ruled by the sun and the element of fire. It is offered to the goddess Hecate in ritual.

Galangal (*Alpinia officinarium*): In Hoodoo magick of the South, this botanical is commonly known as "Little John to Chew." It got this name because it is chewed and spit out in small amounts in an area to distribute it. Having the properties of luck, success, protection, power, and increase, it can be used in a variety of different spells and workings. Mars is its planetary ruler, and it is also connected to the element of air.

Gardenia (*Gardenia spp.*): The most common variety of this little shrub is classified as *Gardenia jasminoides*, in the family Rubiaceae. These blooms are effective not only for love workings, but for protection and stress relief. This plant is ruled by the moon and the element of water. Gardenia flowers are sacred to the orishas Oshún and Yemaya and also Santa Muerte.

Guinea Pepper (*Aframomum melegueta*): Also called ataré, alligator pepper, or grains of paradise, these tiny treasures are used in all different types of magick. It is good for love, lust, and protection. You may use these as an offering to the orisha Yemaya and also the ancestors. They are ruled by the sun and the element of fire.

Hazel (*Corylus spp.*): This magickal tree is sacred to the goddesses Hecate, Brigid, Aphrodite, Arianrhod, Artemis, and Diana. Many have chosen to make ritual tools from its wood. It is said to impart prophecy, wisdom, and divine inspiration. Hazel is owned by the element of air and the sun.

Heather (*Calluna vulgaris*): Heather is ruled by the planet Venus and the element of water. The plant is native to Europe and the Celtic isles. It is considered sacred to the goddess Brigid. Heather is also connected to Mercury and used for beginnings, initiations, self-discovery, weather magick, fairy magick, and knowledge.

Heliotrope (*Heliotropium peruviana*): Used as an offering for the goddess Brigid and the orisha Oshún, this is a beautiful botanical for many different workings. Heliotrope is said to bring abundance, calm, peace, invisibility, love, and joy. It is ruled by the sun and owned by the element of fire.

Hibiscus (*Hibiscus spp.*): Also called sorrel, this lovely plant is the national flower of Jamaica. It is ruled by Venus and the element of water. Hibiscus is great to use in spells for concentration, love, lust, passion, and divination. It is also a primary ingredient in many Obeah workings. In La Regla Lucumi, it is used as an offering for the orishas Oya and Chango.

High John (*Ipomoea jalapa*): A popular ingredient in Hoodoo workings, people use it for justice, eloquence, money, healing, power, love, gambling, legal matters, and just about everything you can imagine. It can be grated or shaved and used in gris-gris bags or sprinkling powders. Some people just carry it whole. It is claimed by the sun and the element of fire. High John can be used as an offering for the loa Maman Brigitte.

Holly (*Ilex spp.*): This plant is offered to the goddess Hel and the gods Thor and Lugh. It is owned by Saturn and the element of fire. There are over four hundred species of this plant. They are said to have the magickal properties of consecration, protection, purity, rebirth, luck, healing, and peace.

Hops (*Humulus lupulus*): Sacred to the goddesses Brigid and Isis, this is primarily used in dream and sleep magick. Some believe it is ruled by the sun, while others assign it the character of the moon. It is also connected to wolves; in fact, its Latin name means wolf. A primary component in brewing, it is associated with the element of water and is used in that aspect in many Native American ceremonies. You may also use it in magick focused on blessings and protection.

Hyacinth (*Hyacinthus orientalis*): Hyacinth is used for everything from chasing away nightmares to granting wishes. It is particularly useful in spells for abundance, good fortune, luck, and protection. Ruled by the planet Venus, this spring flower lends a special blessing of love and joy to your magick. It is used for the orisha Yemaya and is connected to the element of water.

Hyssop (*Hyssopus officinalis*): This is one of those fantastic herbs that blesses us with both medical and magickal benefits. It is known to have medicinal benefits to heal from coughs, and was even sprinkled about in medieval times to keep away the plague. The primary magickal use of hyssop is for purification. Ritual work involving purification should be done whenever you begin anything new, or whenever you feel there is negative fallout from an individual or a situation you are connected with. Most people assign it the planetary correspondence of Jupiter and align it with the element of fire. It is also used as an offering for the orisha Oshún and her father, Obatala.

Irish Moss (*Chondrus crispus*): Despite its name, this actually isn't a moss at all, but rather a species of algae. The plant is sacred to the loa Maman Brigitte and the goddesses Brigid and Aphrodite. It is useful in magick for luck, safe journeys, and protection. Irish moss is ruled by the planet Saturn and the element of water.

Jasmine (*Jasminum officinale*): This plant is also known by the poetic name "moonlight on the grove." It is sacred to the orisha Yemaya, the orixa Pomba Gira, the Voodoo queen Marie Laveau, and the goddesses Hecate, Diana, and Venus. This tiny white flower boasts a beautiful scent. Jasmine is said to bring prophetic dreams, confidence, compassion, grace, peace, rejuvenation, love, and success. Clearly, it can be used in a variety of different spells and offerings. It is ruled by the moon and also the element of water.

Juniper Berries (*Juniperus communis*): These berries are offered to the goddesses Hecate, Astarte, and Ishtar. Juniper berries can be used in spells for love and lust. You can make an infusion out of them and add them to your bath or floor wash to bring about passion and strength. More common, however, is the use of juniper berries for protection and increasing psychic power.

Lavender (*Lavandula angustifolia*): This all-purpose herb is sacred to Lilith, Brigid, Circe, Hecate, Aradia, and many other goddesses. It functions primarily as a strong psychic amplifier, which will add increase and success to all that you do. You can add it to spells for clairvoyance, dream magick, happiness, healing, love, money, and protection. It is associated with the planet Mercury and the element of air.

Lemon (*Citrus limonum*): Ruled by the moon, this is one of the favorite fruits of the orisha Yemaya and the goddesses Juno and Luna. This is used to bring calm, protection, joy, happiness, and love. It is owned by the element of water. You may wish to use the peel, the juice, or the whole fruit as an offering and an ingredient in spells and workings.

Lemon Balm (*Melissa officinalis*): This herb is also sacred to the orisha Yemaya. It is thought to be an aphrodisiac, and can bring about success, protection, and healing, and improve psychic development. Lemon balm is ruled by the moon and the element of water.

Lilac (*Syringa vulgaris*): These beautiful purple blooms are loved by many types of butterflies, as well as the orisha Yemaya and the loa Maman Brigitte. It can be used in divination magick as well as spells for peace, calm, harmony, and wisdom. Lilac is owned by the element of water and the planet Venus.

Lily (*Lilium spp.*): This flower is particularly loved by Juno and Venus, and is therefore useful in workings for relationships, love, and marriage. It can also be used for protection magick, and when honoring the dead. The moon is its ruler along with the element of water.

Lily of the Valley (*Convallaria majalis*): With its tiny white blooms, this is one of my favorite flowers. Also known as May lily or Our Lady's Tears, this flower is sacred to the Norse goddess Freya. It is used in spellwork for happiness and optimism, and also removing negativity. Lily of the valley is ruled by the planet Mercury and the element of air.

Lime (*Citrus spp.*): Limes are used as an offering for the orisha Oya. This useful fruit helps with cleansings, purification, and banishings and also brings loyalty, strength, and friendship. It is governed by the planet Venus and the element of water.

Lotus (*Nelumbo nucifera*): This is used in many different cultures to aid in communication with the higher realms. Ruled by the moon and connected to the element of water, it has special properties for dream workings and astral projection. Lotus is also helpful in workings for divination, meditation, healing, and protection. It is used as an offering to the orishas Yemaya and Oshún and the goddess Isis.

Magnolia (*Magnolia spp.*): One of the most beautiful flowering spring trees, this botanical is used in love magick and workings to bring great joy and lasting peace. It is claimed by the element of earth and ruled by Venus. Much of the lore around this botanical concerns spells regarding fidelity in a relationship. It is also very helpful for purifying a sacred space and removing residual negativity that may be brought about by a person or situation.

Maguey (*Agave americana*): This native Mexican plant was considered highly prized by both the Maya and the Aztecs. Also called the century plant, rattlesnake master, and tree of life, it is a main ingredient in pulque and tequila. Sacred to Santa Muerte, this plant is ruled by Mars and the element of fire.

Marijuana (*Cannabis spp.*): Cannabis has been used religiously in many different cultures. In the Taoist tradition, it was used to communicate with spirits. In Hinduism, it is used in workings for purification and cleansing. In Rastafarianism, it's called ganja and is used for rituals that bring adherents closer to their creator. Marijuana is sometimes given as an offering to Santa Muerte. It is ruled by Saturn and is said to help with spells for love, healing, happiness, inspiration, psychic power, and sexuality.

Mugwort (*Artemisia vulgaris*): Said to vibrate with the energy of the full moon, this herb is sacred to the goddesses Lilith and Hecate. Astrologically it is governed by the planet Venus and the element of water. It is helpful with divination, psychic connection, astral travel, and dream work.

Mullein (*Verbascum thapsus*): One of the few herbs used for Nana Buruku, this herb is said to protect you from almost everything, from wild animals to ghosts to nightmares. Some believe it is ruled by Mercury, while others attach it to Saturn. Water is its ruling element. It was especially prized among indigenous Americans.

Mullein can also be used in spells and workings as a substitute for cemetery dirt.

Musk: Sacred to the goddesses Lilith and Athena, musk was originally derived from the scent glands of an animal. It is used in sex magick, but also to give strength, focus, and determination. It falls under the domain of the sun and Saturn, and the elements of water and fire.

Myrrh (*Commiphora myrrha*): Sacred to Isis, Lilith, Brigid, Hecate, Oya, Cybele, Isis, Juno, and many other divinities, this has been used as a sacred fragrance for thousands of years. Myrrh is not really an herb, but technically a resin that comes from a tree grown in parts of Africa. Myrrh is harvested by cutting into the bark, which then drips out the delightful golden resin, commonly referred to as tears. The tears are used as an incense base for many different magickal formulas. It is considered feminine and is associated primarily with the energy of the moon. Myrrh is known to help balance the root chakra. It also aids in astral travel and meditation by helping with focus. You may also use it for protection, power, luck, transformation, and healing. Elementally it is governed by water.

Myrtle (*Myrtus communis*): This herb is used as an offering for the orisha Oshún and the goddesses Freya, Aphrodite, Cybele, and Venus. In Victorian England it was a symbol of fidelity, and can be used for abundance, money, fertility, luck, and peace. It is ruled by the element of water and the planet Venus.

Nutmeg (*Myristica fragrans*): Ruled by Jupiter and the element of fire, nutmeg is a powerful spice. It is used as an offering to the orisha Oshún. This common kitchen spice is associated with love, relationships, healing, wealth, fidelity, strength, and divination, and is also said to grant psychic visions and intense dreams.

Oak (*Quercus spp.*): The sacred wood is used to honor the goddesses Brigid, Cybele, Cerridwen, and Hecate. Ruled by Jupiter and the element of water, it has the qualities of peace, strength, endurance, focus, justice, spiritual power, prosperity, protection, and bravery.

It is a great material for making ritual tools, as simply carrying this plant is said to grant you good luck.

Oakmoss (*Evernia prunastri*): Oakmoss is a species of lichen. It is used as an offering for the orisha Oya. Earth is its element and it is assigned to the planet Jupiter. Oakmoss is known to grant money, strength, luck, success, and protection.

Orange (*Citrus aurantium dulcis*): Oranges are ruled by the sun and the element of fire. They are used as an offering to the orisha Oshún (in multiples of 5) and the loa Maman Brigitte. Oranges are said to bring energy, abundance, success, love, and joy. They are also helpful with divination and psychic connection. You may wish to add a dried orange peel where you keep your tarot cards or pendulum to capitalize on this ability.

Orchid (*Orchis spp.*): This is said to impart true love, healing, and harmony. It is ruled by Venus and the element of water. There are over one hundred thousand varieties of orchid in the world. One of my favorite things to do is add either the fresh flower or the living plant to altars and shrines to show my love for the goddesses and orishas. Every color of orchid has a slightly different meaning, so choose wisely: Yellow and orange orchids spread joy and happiness. Purple orchids increase psychic connections. White orchids add an air of peace and harmony, and pink orchids are used for love. Orchids are sacred to the orisha Oshún and the goddess Venus.

Orris Root (*Iris germanica*): Orris root is actually the root of an iris flower. It has traditionally been used as a fixative in perfumes and formulas. The plant is ruled by Venus and the element of water. Anyone who has ever grown an iris knows they like it pretty wet. Orris root is used primarily for love, romance, protection, psychic communication, and divination. They are given to the loa Erzulie Freda Dahomey and the goddesses Hera, Aphrodite, and Venus.

Palm (*Arecaceae spp.*): Palm oil is used in many magickal offerings in Africa and the Caribbean. In La Regla Lucumi, palm oil is often used as a substitute for a blood offering, while in Haitian Vodou palm fronds are considered an integral part of the worship of the loa Ayizan. Palms are also considered sacred to the goddess Isis. The plant is said to bring transformation, renewal, clarity, peace, victory, and power to your workings. They are associated with the sun and the element of fire.

Parsley (*Petroselinum crispum*): This herb comes to us from the Mediterranean. It is used for psychic vision, unity, protection for yourself and your home, healing, and courage through difficult transitions. It is under the protection of Venus, Aphrodite, and Persephone, and is given as an offering to the orisha Oshún. Parsley is ruled by the element of air and the planet Mercury.

Passion Flower (*Passiflora spp.*): A whole host of plants in this classification bears this name. They are ruled by the planet Venus and elementally connected to water. They do bring passion to a working, like their name implies, but they also impart a peaceful, calm, and friendly atmosphere. They can be offered to the orisha Yemaya.

Patchouli (*Pogostemon cablin*): The primary use for this herb is in lust and sex magick, but you can also use this to bring prosperity, grounding, and luck, and to remove injustice. It is used as an offering to the goddesses Hecate and Lilith. Their earthy scent is ruled by the element of earth and the planet Jupiter.

Peony (*Paeonia spp.*): This flower is said to dispel negative energy and also bring blessings, luck, fairy gifts, and joy. The red and black seeds are often given as an offering to Pomba Gira and her husband Exú. Strands of the seeds are often worn by devotees of the religion. It is ruled by the sun and the element of fire.

Peppermint (*Mentha piperita*): This type of mint is used for energy work and to bring health and protection against evil. An herb of Mercury and the element of fire, it is used as an offering to many different orisha, but particularly to Nana Buruku.

Poppy (*Papaveraceae spp.*): In accordance with their narcotic properties, this flower has always been associated with dreams and visions.

Red poppies are said to bring pleasure, while yellow ones signify success. They are also used for divination, honoring the dead, and spells dealing with invisibility. Both the flowers and seeds are used to honor the goddesses Hecate, Aphrodite, Persephone, Venus, and Nyx. Poppies are ruled by water and the moon.

Primrose (*Primula vulgaris*): Primrose is associated with the orisha Oshún and the goddesses Freya, Flora, Brigid, Diana, and Bast. Bathing in the herb is said to make one more attractive and beautiful. In Victorian England's language of flowers, this delicate beauty was said to mean "I can't live without you." It brings love and truth. Primrose is ruled by the planet Venus and the element of earth.

Rose (*Rosa spp.*): Roses are by far the most popular flower associated with love. Ritually they are given to Oshún, Yemaya, Pomba Gira, Freya, Hecate, Isis, Santa Muerte and many other representations of the divine feminine. They are said to confer love, joy, and passion on their users. You may choose to use rose water, rose oil, rose petals, or other parts of the plant, claimed by Venus and the element of water, in your magick.

Rosemary (*Rosmarinus officinalis*): The herb, the wood, and the oil of this plant are all used. Rosemary is said to bring protection, healing, purification, strength, clarity, and love. It is used as an offering for Oshún and several of the male orishas. I often place rosemary plants on my windowsill and in my window box to help bless and protect my home. Rosemary is known to be ruled by the sun and the element of fire.

Rue (*Ruta graveolens*): Traditionally it has been used since ancient times for warding off danger, and also creating an atmosphere of protection and healing. Rue is regarded as an herb of bitterness, but also an herb of grace. Astrologically it is associated with the planet Mars, and also the element of fire. It is used as an offering for the goddesses Hel, Hecate, Diana, and Aradia, as well as Santa Muerte. It is invaluable for removing serious blocks, negativity, hexes, and evil.

Saffron (*Crocus sativus*): The modern version of this crocus was probably derived from the wild crocus from Greece. It is sacred to the goddess Hecate. Saffron is said to have healing properties and help relieve depression. Even Queen Cleopatra was said to have used this plant, bathing in it to enhance her beauty and her love life. It is said to help with sex magick, divination, and also financial trouble.

Sage (*Salvia officinalis*): Now that a whole new generation of witches has come out of the broom closet loud and proud, sage is everywhere and honored for the powerful force that it is. It is used for health, blessings, and removing all forms of negative energy most commonly in the form of a smudge stick or sage bundle. Caution should be taken, however, when using around pregnant women and nursing mothers. It is sacred to the goddesses Brigid and Hecate and the orisha Obatala. Sage is owned by the planet Jupiter and the element of air. This herb can help you connect with your spirit animals and guides, and your own power.

Sandalwood (*Santalum album*): Used cross-culturally for protection, purification, psychic connection, joy, and healing, sandalwood is one of the most versatile magickal ingredients around. This resin is burned as an offering to the goddesses Freya and Venus and the orisha Oya. Sandalwood is connected to the element of water and the moon.

Sesame (*Sesamum indicum*): Offered to Hecate, the tiny seeds are known to open doors and locks, hence the phrase "Open Sesame." Both the seeds and the oil are great at attracting healing, money, passionate love, and abundance. It is ruled by the sun and the element of fire.

Spearmint (*Mentha spicata*): In Spanish this plant is called *yerba buena*. Like the other mints, this herb is useful for protection, clarity, psychic knowledge, healing, and spiritual cleansing. It is sacred to the orisha Yemaya and either the leaves or the oil may be used. Spearmint is known to be connected to Venus and the element of water.

Strawberry (*Fragaria ananassa*): These juicy red berries are said to bring joy and blessings to all that you do. They are considered sacred to the goddess Freya and the orisha Oya, and I often leave them as an offering to the dead and the ancestors. You can use them in spellwork for beauty, love, divination, and success. They are associated with the element of water and the planet Venus.

Sunflower (*Helianthus annuus*): Ruled by the sun, sunflowers are devotional gifts to many different gods and goddesses. Adored by everyone from Apollo to Oshún to Incan priestesses, this flower is loved worldwide. They are said to bring joy, energy, self-esteem, healing, luck, courage, wisdom, and special gifts when added to your magick.

Tamarind (*Tamarindus indica*): Offered to the serpent loa Aida Wedo, this herb is ruled by the planet of Saturn and the element of water. Tamarind is said to bring love, healing, and joy.

Tansy (*Tanacetum vulgare*): This native European herb is traditionally offered to the goddess Freya. It is a member of the daisy family that is said to both repel pests and promote good health. Tansy is an herb of immortality and can be used to give your spells long-lasting potency. Tansy also helps with spells of invisibility, longevity, pleasure, and reconciliation. It is ruled by the planet Venus and vibrates with the element of water.

Tarragon (*Artemisia dracunculus*): The goddess Lilith is honored with tarragon. Its name means "little dragon." It is said to grant healing, compassion, love, peace, and protection. Tarragon is ruled by the planet Mercury and the air element.

Thyme (*Thymus vulgaris*): Thyme is a delightful little kitchen herb that you can use for health, loyalty, affection, love, courage, divination, psychic power, and protection. Offerings of thyme can be given to the loa Erzulie Dantor and the orisha Oya. It is associated with the planet Mars and the element of fire.

Tobacco (*Nicotiana spp.*): There are over seventy known species of this plant sacred to the orixa Pomba Gira and the goddess Hecate. Many are familiar with tobacco as an offering in many Native

American traditions representing spiritual connection, protection, guidance, and healing. In traditional Hoodoo and Conjure workings it can be used in spells of controlling, compelling, and also banishing. Tobacco is ruled by the planet Mars and the element of fire.

Tulip (*Tulipa spp.*): These delightful flowers are said to bring luck, good fortune, fertility, love, prosperity, success, and psychic messages. They can be used as an offering to Santa Muerte. Tulips are ruled by the planet Jupiter, and the element of earth.

Vanilla (*Vanilla planifolia*): This delicious bean comes to us from a species of orchid and can be used in your kitchen magick and elsewhere. Vanilla is known for having the properties of beauty, clarity, communication, healing, love, joy, prophecy, personal empowerment, and energy. It is used as an offering to the orisha Oshún and the goddess Hecate. Like all the other orchids, vanilla is ruled by the planet Venus and the element of water.

Vetiver (*Chrysopogon zizanioides*): Used as an offering for the goddesses Hel, Aphrodite, and Venus, this earthy scent is said to grant protection and courage. In fact, vetiver is associated with the element of earth and the sign Taurus. It is said to have a calming and clearing effect on your body and your space. Vetiver can also bring abundance, good fortune, prosperity, and luck to your workings.

Violet (*Viola odorata*): Used as an offering to the goddesses Brigid, Cybele, Aphrodite, and Venus, violets appear in spells for luck, wishes, peace, healing, protection, and absorbing evil. Ancient Greeks used these flowers to promote peaceful sleep and beneficial dreams. Violets are connected to the planet Venus and the element of water.

Wild Cherry (*Prunus avium*): Parts of this tree are used as an offering for the goddesses Freya, Guanyin (Kwan Yin), and Aphrodite. It is known to open doors, remove blockages, and grant special favors, and to foster love, healing, and compassion. The planet Venus and the element of air is said to control this tree.

Willow (*Salix spp.*): In actuality there are over four hundred species of tree that are called willow. They are water-loving beings that often have roots even larger than their limbs and trunk. They are sacred to both the goddesses Hecate, Brigid, Artemis, Diana, Persephone, and the loa Maman Brigitte. Willow is connected to the moon and is said to help with psychic dreams, divination, empathy, enchantment, astral travel, divination, grief, and healing. Willow is also known to provide gentle love and calm. It is particularly useful for making ritual wands and other tools. Willow is ruled elementally by water.

Wormwood (*Artemisia absinthium*): Many are familiar with the herb as the primary ingredient in absinthe. This herb is used as an offering for the goddesses Hel, Artemis, Isis, and Lakshmi, and the loa Aida Wedo. It is helpful with astral travel, courage, dream work, divination, and protection from negative energy. Mars is its governing planet and it falls under the element of fire.

Yarrow (*Achillea millefolium*): The name of this lovely plant means "a thousand leaves." It is ruled by Venus and has been found in archaeological sites dating back over sixty thousand years. These flowers are considered sacred to the goddesses Freya and Hel and the orisha Oshún. Yarrow stalks and flowers are used in magick for divination, prophecy, banishing, purification, love, marriage, and healing. It is especially helpful when used for psychic protection against negative people and destructive influences. Yarrow is ruled by the element of water.

Yew (*Taxus baccata*): Offered to the goddesses Hel and Hecate, this is a plant of transformations. It allows for connection to your ancestors, psychic visions, mediumship, healing, and hope. It is associated with the planet Pluto and the element of water.

Ylang-Ylang (*Cananga odorata*): Sometimes referred to as the "flower of flowers," this powerful floral is known for bringing passion, love, calm, abundance, foresight, opportunity, and irresistible qualities to your magick. Most often, people use this in essential oil form. It is considered a sacred offering for the orisha Oshún. It is ruled by Venus and the element of water and therefore will make a good addition to ritual baths.

Appendix B

SACRED DIRTS AND CRYSTALS

African traditional religions are more likely to include the use of sacred dirts in their offerings and magickal creations than they are crystals. It is almost as if crystals can give off a more generalized earth-based foundation and therefore can be used in a variety of situations rather than being the sole domain of a single orisha or energy. In keeping with this, this list contains both of these items so you can best use these earth elements in your workings.

Amber: Technically, amber is a resin. It comes from ancient sap that has solidified over time. Because of its hardness, many practitioners treat it as a crystal or stone. Amber beads are frequently used in ritual jewelry for the goddesses Freya and Artemis and the orisha Oshún. Ruled by the element of water, it is used in both balancing and energizing workings, as well as for love and healing.

Carnelian: This is a stone of energy, courage, and success. It is given as an offering to the goddess Brigid and can be useful for healing past struggles or depression.

Citrine: Sacred to the goddess Freya, this is a stone of wealth, abundance, great joy, and success. Also called cairngorm, it is good for encouraging creativity and boosting self-esteem. If you are feeling uncertain, it is a good stone to carry to help remove fears and negative emotions.

Dirt from a Cemetery: Cemetery dirt is used to connect with and honor the ancestors. It is also used in hexing and protection magick. Be sure to leave an offering when collecting this dirt. Dirt specifically from the oldest female grave in a particular cemetery is sacred to Maman Brigitte in Haitian Vodou and New Orleans Voodoo.

Dirt from a Footprint: This dirt is used when you are doing a working on a specific person—namely, whomever's footprint you have. I've seen this as a primary ingredient in love spells, and also spells of commanding or compelling. It is also frequently used in spellwork for Santa Muerte. The normal practice is to gather up the footprint dirt and place it in a paper bag. Please remember to consider the ethics of doing workings like these before you begin. I would never use someone's footprint dirt without their prior permission.

Dirt from the Crossroads: Crossroads dirt is known to bring blessings of success, guidance, clarity, and opportunity. It is sacred to the crossroads deities: Eleggua, Legba, Eshu, Pomba Gira, Hecate, and many others. For best results, leave an offering of three or twenty-one pennies, or something more valuable, when you harvest your dirt.

Dirt from Your Home: Dirt from your home is a simple way to begin using dirt in your magickal spells. This dirt represents "spirit of place" and will stand in for your home and the people who live there in any magickal workings you do. I have also known practitioners who use the sweepings from their floor to stand in for dirt when they live in a location that doesn't feature a yard. You may add this to any of the gris-gris bag recipes in this book to help personalize them and make them specifically geared to you.

Garnet: It's no wonder this deep red stone of love and passion is sacred to Lilith. It was originally used in wedding rings long before diamonds became popular. It is also a stone of regeneration and focus, which will help grant your workings energy and power. Garnet is also famous for help with release of unnecessary emotions and situations. You may consider carrying one with you when you are going to face a difficult task.

Jade: Sacred to the goddess Brigid and the loa Maman Brigitte, this stone has been highly prized since ancient times. It is said to open the heart chakra and make you more grounded, stabilized, and relaxed.

Jet: In many different traditions of witchcraft, necklaces of amber and jet were seen as the mark of a high priestess. Jet in all its dark majesty, it is sacred to the goddess Lilith. It is prized for its ability to transform a negative situation. The stone operates as an energy filter that has supreme protection and purification ability. Some even use jet to clean and clear other stones. It also features a wonderful quality of centering and grounding to those who wear it or carry it with them.

Moonstone: Ruled by the divine feminine power of the moon, moonstone is sacred to the goddesses Freya, Hecate, Hel, and Brigid. It is known to have the magickal properties of increasing psychic ability and granting calm and healing.

Onyx: Sacred to the goddesses Venus, Hel, Hecate, and Lilith, this black stone is said to heal trauma in this life or previous ones. Onyx is believed to promote energy, endurance, and learning, and also to relieve stress. This stone is even mentioned in the Bible as a stone of creation. It has long been used for offering and ceremony, and may also be used for scrying, divination, past-life work, and mediumship.

Tourmaline (Black): This is used for the goddess Aradia, and also can be used in conjunction with the dark goddesses Lilith and Hecate and the loa Maman Brigitte. Black tourmaline is said to remove negative energy and grant healing and a positive attitude and atmosphere.

Turquoise: This is used as an offering for the orisha Yemaya. It gives love, healing, joy, luck, and longevity to its user.

Appendix C

SACRED SYMBOLS

Many divine symbols used for the sacred feminine forces are discussed in this book. They can be carved on candles, drawn on the earth, crafted as veves, recreated on your altars and shrines, embroidered on flags or clothing, or carried as a talisman. The possibilities are almost endless.

Crescent moon: Many different energies can be symbolized by the crescent moon. It is an aspect of the orisha Yemaya and the goddesses Brigid and Diana.

Crossroads: The crossroads is a space of in-between; it is where the magick literally happens. In African traditional religions these are spaces for Legba, Eleggua, or Pomba Gira, the guardians of possibility. Crossroads are also the domain of the goddess Hecate.

Dark moon Lilith symbol: This symbol comes to us from astrology and is used to embody all the elements the dark moon Lilith represents.

Heart: The heart is used as a symbol for Freya, the orisha Oshún, and many of the Erzulie loas.

Panos: In Santeria, sometimes ritual coverings are created to blanket various orisha shrines or ritual items. These are called *panos,* which literally means "cloth" in Spanish. Very often these are beaded, embroidered, or painted with the symbols of the orisha. For example, a Yemaya pano will feature cowrie shells or waves, while an Oshún one might feature bees or butterflies.

Pontos: "Points" used in the Brazilian traditions of Candomble and Umbanda. Many of these are used for Exu and his wife Pomba Gira. These very often contain crossroads or pitchforks, both symbolic of these divinities.

Venus: This is another symbol borrowed from astrology, which has been evocative of the divine feminine womb since ancient times.

Veves: Traditionally, veves are unique creations that are drawn on the ground in flour or cornmeal to salute the loa in Haitian Vodou. Over time, these have been adapted to become inscribed on jewelry, used as tattoos (hopefully with respect and caution), and carved into candles. Just like their use has evolved over time, so has their form. It is almost as if no two veves are ever the same. Each drawing is susceptible to both the interpretation and execution of the artist creating it, and also where they are creating it. There are some commonalities that have been handed down throughout the years. Erzulie Freda is most often honored with a veve shaped like a heart filled with a lattice. Erzulie Danto's veve almost always features a dagger or a sword in addition to the sacred heart. Alternatively, the veve for Damballa and Aida Wedo most often feature intertwined snakes, which hearkens back to the mythology surrounding these two divine beings. The veve for Maman Brigitte very often features a tombstone, similar to the veves used for her husband, Baron Samedi.

GLOSSARY

When I began writing this book, I did not intend to add a glossary. However, it quickly became clear that both pronunciation and meaning can get confusing when discussing the manifestations of orishas, loas, and queens throughout the world. Pronunciation of some of these words can be tricky and while I am by no means a linguist, I have attempted to elucidate some of these words and concepts here.

21 Divisions: A variety of African traditional religion practiced primarily in the Dominican Republic.

African Diaspora: Refers to the dispersal of Africans throughout the world, either voluntarily or involuntarily.

African Traditional Religions: African-based religious beliefs that are neither Christian nor Islamic. They are known to include La Regla Lucumi, Ifa, Vodou, Voodoo, Candomble, Umbanda, 21 Divisions, Obeah, and others.

Ashé/Axé/Ase (AH-Shay): The universal life force. It can also be an exclamation meaning, "So be it."

Awo (AH-woh): That which is looked into or through, or a mystery. It also means spiritual knowledge. The word is most often used to refer to a priest in the tradition, as in the word *babalawo*.

Baba (BAH-bah): A term of respect in African traditional religions, it can be used as the shortened form of babalawo, or to mean father.

Babalawo (Bah-bah-lah-woh): Priest of Orunla in the La Regla Lucumi and Ifa faiths.

Bon Dye/ Bondye (Bone-die): Literally translating to "Good God," they are seen as the supreme deity in Haitian Vodou.

Boutey (Boo-tay): A ritual bottle in Haitian Vodou.

Boveda (Bow-vay-dah): An ancestor shrine or space in La Regla Lucumi.

Candomble: An African traditional religion practiced primarily in Brazil.

Congo (kän-go): A name for the Arada/Dahomey line of loa in Haitian Vodou.

Dahomey (duh-hoh-mee): A West African kingdom in place until the late nineteenth century. It is now part of Benin.

Divine Feminine: Sacred feminine forces present both in the universe and oneself, regardless of gender.

Drapo (drä-pö): The ritual flags of Haitian Vodou. These are created by devotees and used to represent the Ashe of the loa in ritual.

Egun/Egungun (Eh-goon): The Yoruba word for ancestor(s).

Erzulie/Ezili (ER-Zool-eh or Eeee-zeel-eee): A group of loa in Haitian Vodou. Erzulie Freda, Erzulie Danto, and Maitresse Erzulie are all part of her Ashe.

Florida Water: A cologne whose primary ingredients are lemon, bergamot, and cinnamon in an alcohol base.

Gede/Guedeh (GAY-day): The group of the spirits of the dead in Haitian Vodou. Some say this represents only the unknown dead, while others include in the group all who have passed.

God/Goddess: The divine beings in the visible and invisible world.

Hoodoo (HOO-doo): Southern U.S. folk magick practices that are loosely based on African traditional religions.

Hounfor/Ounfò (Hoon-four): Ritual temple or sacred site of Haitian Vodou.

Houngan/Oungan (Hoon-gan): A Haitian Vodou or New Orleans Voodoo priest. Linguistically it comes from the Fon words, which mean spirit and chief.

Ifa (E-fah): This is the name of an orisha who controls divination and the West African Yoruba religion itself as it is practiced today.

Iya (E-yah): Term of respect given to priestesses in the African traditional religions; roughly translates to "mother."

La Regla Lucumi/Lucumi (Lew-cu-mee): The Cuban name for the African traditional religious practices that flourish there. It is mistakenly more commonly known as Santeria.

Lavé Tet (Lah-veh-tet): Ceremony in Haitian Vodou to baptize and welcome someone into the tradition. It literally translates to "wash head."

Loa/Lwa (Low-WA): The deities or spirits of Haitian Vodou and New Orleans Voodoo.

Loup-Garou (loo-Gah-roo): A shapeshifting being similar to a werewolf.

Maman Brigitte/Gran Brigitte: A wise loa in the traditions of Haitian Vodou and New Orleans Voodoo who is very often seen as a foremother.

Mambo/Manbo (Mom-bow): A Haitian Vodou or New Orleans Voodoo priestess. Customarily this title is conferred after one receives the asson, or ritual rattle, as part of an initiation.

Mami Wata: An ancient and powerful creator deity who is the embodiment of water.

Mojuba (Mow-joo-ba): This word means, "Thanks and praise"; it is also used as an honoring meaning "I salute you."

Moon: The celestial body that is known to affect the visible and invisible world. The full moon is said to be a most advantageous time for performing workings, while the new moon is specifically helpful for spells and rituals to bring new situations into your life.

Mother Goddess: A creator deity who most often has traditionally maternal attributes.

Nana Buruku (Nan-ah Brr-oo-coo): A Lucumi and Ifa maternal deity representing female courage, knowledge, and power.

New Orleans Voodoo: The Louisiana-based variety of African traditional religion. It incorporates many different practices from throughout the world.

Oba (Oh-bah): One of the wives of the orisha Chango in the Lucumi and Ifa religions. She is said to have cut off her ears.

Obeah (Oh-bey-yuh): The Jamaican-based variety of African traditional religion.

Ocha (Oh-chah): A shortened variation of the word *orisha*. Sometimes the entire religion is also referred to as Ocha, and you will hear people say they are "in Ocha."

Olodumare (Oh-low-doo-MAR-ray)/Olorun (oh-loh-ROON): Creator deity in La Regla Lucumi.

Olokun (Oh-low-koon): The orisha representing the depths of the ocean. They are androgynous and seen as a counterpart to the orisha Yemaya.

Oracle: A priestess or priest who delivers psychic messages from the Divine.

Orisha/Orixa (O-REE-Sha): This word roughly translates to "owner of the spirit of the head" in the Yoruba language. It is used in Ifa, La Regla Lucumi, Candomble, and other African traditional religions to mean the deities in the traditions.

Oshún/Osun/Ochun/Oxum (Oh-shoon): The spirit of the Ashe of the river. She is said to preside over matters of love, fertility, marriage, dance, and money.

Oya (Oi-yah): This orisha represents the Ashe of the wind. She is present in Africa and also in the Cuban tradition of La Regla Lucumi.

Palo (PAH-low): Also known as Palo Monte or Palo Mayombe, this is a Congo-derived manifestation of African traditional religion.

Pataki (Pah-tak-e): The ritual stories of La Regla Lucumi. They are told as part of divination, and to help people better understand the many faces of the orisha.

Petro (Pet-row): This is one of the lines, or branches, of Haitian Vodou. It is often associated with fire.

Pomba Gira (pō-ba xira): A group of Brazilian orixas who are said to rule crossroads and transformation.

Poto Mitan (Po-toe-mit-on): The ritual centerpole in Haitian Vodou. The loa are said to travel up and down this pole as they pass through the realm of the living. Veves are also drawn around it.

Rada (Rah-dah): This is one of the lines, or branches, of Haitian Vodou. They are said to most often manifest as cool or gentle spirits.

Santeria (san-teh-rēa): The common name given to the worship of the saints and African traditional religious practices taking place in Cuba and Puerto Rico. It is more properly referred to as La Regla Lucumi, or La Regla de Ocha (The Rule of Ocha).

Santero/Santera (san-teh-row/san-teh-rah): The priest and priestess of the La Regla Lucumi religion. They have been initiated or crowned with their ruling orisha.

Tarot (tah-row): A system of divination using seventy-eight cards that originated in the fifteenth century.

Umbanda: Variety of African traditional religion practiced primarily in Brazil. It often incorporates some indigenous rites and practices.

Veve (vey-vey): This is a sacred drawing for the loa. Most often it is a ground drawing made of cornmeal or flour. It can be created to represent a single loa or combined to salute an entire group of energies.

Vodou/Vodun (Vo-dou): The Haitian manifestation of African traditional religion. Some theorize that the word is from the Dahomey people and means simply "deity," or that sacred thing which is outside ourselves.

Vodousaint (Vo-dou-san): Practitioners of Haitian Vodou.

Voodoo (VOO-doo): The most common word used for the New Orleans variation of African traditional religion.

Yanvalou (YAN-va-loo): A dance and drum rhythm used in Haitian Vodou and New Orleans Voodoo.

Yemaya/Yemayá/Iemanja/Yemonja/Janaína: The orisha in African traditional religions who represents the Ashe of water.

Yeye (YAY-yay): Term of respect given to priestesses in La Regla Lucumi that roughly translates to "mother."

RECOMMENDED RESOURCES AND READINGS

Resources

The New Orleans Voodoo Spiritual Temple, located at 1428 North Rampart Street, New Orleans, Louisiana 70116 (voodoo spiritualtemple.org). Priestess Miriam has run this sacred site for over twenty-eight years. Started in concert with her late husband, Oswan Chamani, the Temple provides spiritual healings, services, readings, and products for absolutely every spiritual need. This has been my spiritual home for most of my adult life, and I am proud and grateful to be a part of the family there.

The Caribbean Cultural Center, located at 120 East 125th Street, New York, New York 10035 (www.cccadi.org). This is one of the most valuable resources we have here in New York City. Their mission, as stated on their website, is one that "preserves and presents African Diaspora cultures; trains the next generation of cultural leaders; and unites Diaspora communities. We leverage arts and culture as tools for personal transformation, community-building, and social justice."

Mystery School of the Goddess (mysteryschoolofthegoddess.net). This site provides online workshops and instruction about all aspects of the goddess. I have a few classes featured on this site focusing on magick, crystals, and goddess worship.

Patheos Pagan Blogs (www.patheos.com/pagan). I have been a blogger at Patheos Pagan since 2013. They are the top Pagan blog site in the world. My blog, Voodoo Universe, is now the largest ATR blog in the world. It has consistently provided accurate and respectful information about African Traditional Religions since it began.

Readings

This comprehensive list contains many of the best books on loas, orishas, and goddesses available. There is much erroneous information circulating on the internet and elsewhere about these topics, so if you need something to read, please consider the following works.

Abimbola, Wande. *Yoruba Divination Poetry.* London, England: Nok Publishers, 1977.

Bascom, William. *African Folktales in the New World.* Bloomington: Indiana University Press, 1992.

Beckwith, Martha Warren. *Black Roadways: A Study of Jamaican Folklife.* Greenwich, CT: Negro Universities Press, 1969.

Brown, Karen McCarthy. *Mama Lola: A Vodou Priestess in Brooklyn.* Los Angeles: University of California Press, 1991.

Cabrera, Lydia. *Yemaya y Ochún: Kariocha, Iyalorichas y Olorichas.* Miami, FL: ED. Universal, 1996.

Chestnut, R. Andrew. *Devoted to Death: Santa Muerte, the Skeleton Saint.* Oxford, UK: Oxford University Press, 2018.

Crosley, Reginald. *The Vodou Quantum Leap: Alternative Realities, Power, and Mysticism.* Woodbury, MN: Llewellyn Publications, 2000.

De La Torre, Miguel A. *Santeria: The Beliefs and Ritual of a Growing Religion in America.* Grand Rapids, MI: William B. Eerdmans Publishing Company, 2004.

Deren, Maya. *Divine Horseman.* New York: Thames and Hudson, 1953

Dorsey, Lilith. *The African-American Ritual Cookbook.* Self-published, 1998.

Dorsey, Lilith. *Love Magic: Over 250 Spells and Potions for Getting It, Keeping It, and Making It Last.* Newburyport, MA: Weiser Books, 2016.

Dorsey, Lilith. *Voodoo and Afro-Caribbean Paganism.* New York: Citadel, 2005.

Drewal, Henry John. *Mami Wata: Arts for Water Spirits in Africa and Its Diaspora.* Los Angeles: Fowler Museum at UCLA, 2008.

Dunham, Katherine. *Dances of Haiti.* Los Angeles: University of California Center for Afro-American Studies, 1983.

Dunham, Katherine. *Island Possessed.* Chicago: University of Chicago Press, 1969.

Fleurant, Gerdés. *Dancing Spirits: Rhythms and Rituals of Haitian Vodun, the Rada Rite.* Westport, CT: Greenwood Press, 1996.

Flores-Pena, Ysamur, and Roberta J. Evanchuk. *Santeria Garments and Altars.* Jackson, MS: University Press of Mississippi, 1994.

Girouard, Tina. *Sequin Artists of Haiti.* New Orleans: Contemporary Arts Center of New Orleans, 1994.

Glassman, Sallie Ann. *Vodou Visions.* New York: Villard Books, 2000.

Gleason, Judith. *Oya: In Praise of an African Goddess.* San Francisco: Harper San Francisco, 1992.

Gordon, Leah. *The Book of Vodou.* Hauppauge, NY: Baron's Educational Services, 2000.

Gottlieb, Karla. *The Mother of Us All: A History of Queen Nanny, Leader of the Windward Jamaican Maroons.* Trenton, NJ: Africa World Press, 2000.

Gray, John. *Ashe, Traditional Religion and Healing in Sub-Saharan Africa and the Diaspora: A Classified International Bibliography.* Westport, CT: Greenwood Press, 1988.

Harris, Jessica B. *Iron Pots and Wooden Spoons.* New York: Simon and Schuster, 1999.

Huggens, Kim, ed. *Memento Mori.* London, England: Avalonia Books, 2012.

Hurbon, Laënnec. *Voodoo: Search for the Spirit.* New York : Harry N. Abrams, 1995.

Hurston, Zora Neale. *Mules and Men.* Philadelphia: J. B. Lippincott, 1935.

Hurston, Zora Neale. *Tell My Horse: Voodoo and Life in Haiti and Jamaica.* Philadelphia: J. B. Lippincott, 1938.

Huxley, Francis. *The Invisibles: Voodoo Gods in Haiti.* New York: McGraw Hill, 1966.

Jodorowsky, Alejandro. *Psychomagic: The Transformative Power of Shamanic Psychotherapy.* Rochester, VT: Inner Traditions, 2010.

Johnson, Janet P. *Keelboat Annie: An African-American Legend.* New York: Troll Communications, 1997.

Johnson, Jerah. *Congo Square in New Orleans.* New Orleans: Louisiana Landmarks Society, 1995.

Johnson, Paul Christopher. *Secrets, Gossip, and Gods: The Transformation of Brazilian Candomble.* Oxford, England: Oxford University Press, 2002.

Koltuv, Barbara Black. *The Book of Lilith.* York Beach, ME: Nicolas-Hays, Inc., 1986.

Kristos, Kyle. *Voodoo.* New York: J. B. Lippincott, 1976.

Largey, Michael. *Vodou Nation: Haitian Art, Music, and Cultural Nationalism.* Chicago: University of Chicago Press, 2006.

Leafar, Elhoim. *The Magical Art of Crafting Charm Bags: 100 Mystical Formulas for Success, Love, Wealth, and Wellbeing.* Newburyport, MA: Weiser Books, 2017.

Long, Carolyn Morrow. *Spiritual Merchants: Religion, Magic and Commerce.* Knoxville : University of Tennessee Press, 2001.

Long, Carolyn Morrow. *A New Orleans Voodoo Priestess: The Legend and Reality of Marie Laveau.* Gainesville: University Press of Florida, 2006.

Martinie, Louis. *Dr. John Montanee: A Grimoire.* New Orleans: Black Moon Publishing, 2014.

Martinie, Louis, and Sallie Ann Glassman. *The New Orleans Voodoo Tarot.* Rochester, VT: Destiny Books, 1992.

Mason, Michael Atwood. *Living Santeria: Rituals and Experiences in an Afro-Cuban Religion.* Washington, DC: Smithsonian Books, 2002.

Montenegro, Carlos. *Santeria Magical Formulary & Spellbook.* Plainview, NY: Original Publications, 1994.

Nascimento, Abdias. *The Orixas: Afro-Brazilian Paintings and Text.* Middletown, CT: Afro-American Institute, Wesleyan University, 1969.

Nunez, Luis M. *Santeria: A Practical Guide to Afro-Caribbean Magic.* Washington, DC: Spring Publications, 1992.

Olmos, Margarite Fernandez, and Lizabeth Paravisini-Gerbert. *Creole Religions of the Caribbean.* New York: New York University Press, 2011.

Olupona, Jacob K., and Roland O. Abiodun, eds. *Ifa Divination, Power, and Performance.* Bloomington: Indiana University Press, 2016.

Otero, Solimar, and Toyin Falola, eds. *Yemoja: Gender, Sexuality, and Creativity in the Latina/o and Afro-Atlantic Diasporas.* Albany: State University of New York Press, 2013.

Paton, Diana. *The Cultural Politics of Obeah.* Cambridge, UK: Cambridge University Press, 2015.

Quinones, Ayoka Wiles. *I Hear Olofi's Song.* Philadelphia: Oshún Publishing Company, 2010.

Ramos, Obá Oriaté Miguel "Willie," and Ilarí Obá. *Adimú: Gbogbó Tén'unjé Lukumí.* N.p.: Eleda.org Publications, 2012.

Ribeiro de Souza, Jose. *400 Pontos Riscados e Cantados no Umbanda e Candomble.* Rio de Janeiro, Brazil: Editora Eco, 1966.

Rigaud, Milo. *Ve-Ve: Diagrammes Rituels Du Voudou.* New York: French and European Publications, 1992.

Rigaud, Odette M., Alfred Métraux, and Rhoda Métraux. "The Feasting of the Gods in Haitian Vodu." *Primitive Man* 19, no. 1/2 (January–April 1946): 1–58.

Seneca, Lucius Annaeus. *Complete Works of Seneca the Younger.* Translated by Frank Justus Miller. East Sussex, United Kingdom: Delphi Classics, 2014.

Smith, Michael P. *Spirit World: Pattern in the Expressive Folk Culture of Afro-American New Orleans.* New Orleans: New Orleans Urban Folklife Society, 1984.

Soyinka, Wole. *Myth, Literature, and the African World.* Cambridge, England: Cambridge University Press, 1976.

Teish, Luisah. *Jambalaya: The Natural Woman's Book of Personal Charms and Practical Rituals.* New York: HarperCollins, 1985.

Thompson, Robert Farris. *Flash of the Spirit.* New York: Vintage, 1983.

Washington, Joseph R. *Black Sects and Cults.* New York: Anchor Books, 1972.

Wilcken, Lois. *The Drums of Voodoo.* Tempe, AZ: White Cliffs Media, 1992.

Williams, Sheldon. *Voodoo and the Art of Haiti.* London: Morland Lee, 1969.

Witchdoctor Utu. *Conjuring Harriet "Mama Moses" Tubman and the Spirits of the Underground Railroad.* Newburyport, MA: Weiser Books, 2019.

ABOUT THE AUTHOR

Lilith Dorsey, MA, hails from many magickal traditions including Afro-Caribbean, Celtic, and Native American spirituality. Her more traditional education focused on plant science, anthropology, and film at the University of Rhode Island, New York University, and the University of London, while her magickal training included numerous initiations in Santeria, also known as Lucumi, Haitian Vodoun, and New Orleans Voodoo. She currently runs her own spiritual group called House of Maman Brigitte.

Lilith Dorsey is a Voodoo Priestess and, in that capacity, has been doing successful magick for clients since 1991. She is editor/publisher of *Oshun-African Magickal Quarterly*, creator of the popular blog *Voodoo Universe*, filmmaker of the experimental documentary *Bodies of Water: Voodoo Identity and Tranceformation*, and the author of *Voodoo and Afro-Caribbean Paganism*, *The African-American Ritual Cookbook*, and *Love Magic*. One of her most treasured times was spent as lead choreographer and dancer for jazz legend Dr. John's "Night Tripper" Voodoo Show.

TO OUR READERS

Weiser Books, an imprint of Red Wheel/Weiser, publishes books across the entire spectrum of occult, esoteric, speculative, and New Age subjects. Our mission is to publish quality books that will make a difference in people's lives without advocating any one particular path or field of study. We value the integrity, originality, and depth of knowledge of our authors.

Our readers are our most important resource, and we appreciate your input, suggestions, and ideas about what you would like to see published.

Visit our website at *www.redwheelweiser.com* to learn about our upcoming books and free downloads, and be sure to go to *www.redwheelweiser.com/newsletter* to sign up for newsletters and exclusive offers.

You can also contact us at *info@rwwbooks.com* or at

Red Wheel/Weiser, LLC
65 Parker Street, Suite 7
Newburyport, MA 01950